THE MACHINE AND THE WORKER

THE MACHINE

AND

THE WORKER

ALFRED BARRATT BROWN
Former Principal of Ruskin College
Oxford

With a Foreword
by Mike Cooley

SPOKESMAN
Nottingham

First published in 1934.
This edition published in 2014 by agreement.

Spokesman
Russell House
Bulwell Lane
Nottingham NG6 0BT
England

Phone 0115 9708318
Fax 0115 9420433
www.spokesmanbooks.com

A catalogue record is available from the British Library.

ISBN 978 0 85124 838 7

Printed in Nottingham by Russell Press (www.russellpress.com).

CONTENTS

FOREWORD

This is one of the most interesting, informative and insightful books I have encountered on this topic. It is both cautionary and inspirational.

The author, Alfred Barratt Brown, sees the book as

'a sober analysis of the trend of events in modern industry, in the light of which it may be possible to judge what measures may be required to safeguard us against the disastrous consequences of a machine civilization that shall have forgotten man.'

That is a laudable aspiration but one which needs to be fulfilled more urgently than ever.

Although it was published in 1934 when the author was Principal of Ruskin College, Oxford, its great strength is that it still provides a multidisciplinary framework in which to consider how to progress further the matters addressed. It shows the need to campaign for socially useful systems in an era of exponential technological change, when the gap between technology's potential and its reality becomes a yawning chasm.

Those initiating technological change usually provide an account of its positive features only. History shows, however, that it is a double-edged affair, a form of Faustian exchange. The author deals deftly with this by providing a sort of balance sheet of the gains and losses of such systems.

The author reminds us that in Mary Shelley's story, the monster (Victor) threatens Frankenstein with the words

'Slave! remember that I have power … You are my creator, but I am your master – obey!'

There is an entire chapter devoted to Scientific Management and Labour, also known as Taylorism after the inventor of the system. In its wider application, it provides a further extension of control and subordination of the worker to the machine through Time and Motion control.

There are those who feel that these problems of the human/system interface apply only to manual workers, assuming clerical and administrative staff to be immune. However, the evidence all around shows the contrary.

Managements showed much interest in implementing these systems but frequently the underlying motive was clear. Thus in *The Engineer* (14.09.1978 pp.24-25) we find the statement 'People are trouble but Machines obey', and then in economic papers such as *The Economist* (14.07.1973 p.11) it proclaims 'Robots don't strike'.

The final chapter, entitled 'The Ultimate Question', reminds us

> 'The greatest need of all is the preparation of the mind and spirit that shall refine our standards of judgment and our taste, reverse our false values and purify and simplify our desires.'

This is indeed a *tour de force* and is written in a form that makes it not only accessible but a delightful read. It should be widely read and discussed, not least in departments of engineering and design, as works of this kind are surely as important as mathematical or machine theory.

The Barratt Brown family are to be thanked for making this book available for republication, and Spokesman Books should also be thanked for making it a reality.

Mike Cooley
June 2014

PREFACE

For some years past I have been occupied in the intervals of other work with the subjects that are discussed in this book. Under the title *Man and the Machine* I gave a series of Dunkin Lectures at Manchester College, Oxford, seven years ago. Since then I have spoken and written on one or other aspect of the question on many occasions, including a course of lectures at Mary Ward Settlement in the winter of 1932–1933 under the auspices of the London University Extension Board.

I have not been primarily concerned to suggest remedies but to assess the facts and especially the psychological facts. These are not easy to come by : but to propose remedies without some understanding of them would seem to be singularly pointless. There is a disposition to say that all would be well if we secured a more equitable distribution of purchasing power and of the time spent in work. These are clearly desirable objects : and to realise them would doubtless be to have solved the most important among our economic problems ; but we should still have on our hands a psychological and an ethical problem. For we might distribute more successfully the wealth produced, but still at an intolerable human cost to the producer. Those who put forward projects for a new economic order or a planned society too seldom give attention to the question of the place of machinery and its effect upon the worker's life.

I am not an economist, but I hope that this excursion on the borderlines of psychology and economics will not be resented by those who have a better right on parts of the ground which is covered. I have no practical experience of industry : but I have enjoyed the privilege of the friendship of some hundreds of working men and women who have talked to me of their life and work freely and without conventional reserve. In order that I might have a collection of first-hand records of experience, I have asked a number of workers (including several of my own students at Ruskin College) to set down their personal impressions on various points upon which I questioned them. The bulk of these records come from my own students, but I have also a number from men and women whom I have never met, to whom I am especially indebted for their accounts of the jobs in which they are engaged. I did not question this group of people with a view to any statistical enquiry, for which a far wider and more careful investigation would have to be made : I only aimed at getting some typical reactions to modern industry from workers who are drawn from many different occupations and localities, and who, although most of them are adult students and therefore more thoughtful and articulate than their fellow workers, do I believe represent a much larger body of experience and opinion. I wish to thank them for their readiness to answer my questions and to allow me to make liberal use of their replies.

I have to thank the Editor of the *Hibbert Journal* for permission to reproduce material from three articles contributed to the Journal (in October, 1929, in April, 1930, and in April, 1933).

Finally, I wish to thank Miss Phyllis Groves (now Mrs. Ivor Thomas) for her assistance in preparing the manuscript for the press.

A. Barratt Brown.

Ruskin College, Oxford,
Mayday, 1934.

CHAPTER I

INTRODUCTORY

In 1816 Mary Shelley wrote *Frankenstein : or the Modern Prometheus.* The Shelleys were staying by the Lake of Geneva not far from Lord Byron, and one evening, after Byron had suggested that they should beguile a rainy week by writing each a ghost story, the talk had turned on galvanism and on the possibilities of creating life out of matter. Mary had a waking dream of a student of un-hallowed arts at work on the manufacture of a living being. " I saw the hideous phantasm of a man stretched out, and then, on the working of some powerful engine, show signs of life and stir with an uneasy, half vital motion." On this dream she wrote her story. Probably neither she nor Lord Byron, to whom she read it, realised that it was an allegory of the possible effect on human life of the mechanical inventions that were then beginning to transform the world of industry. Yet, four years before, Byron had made his maiden speech in the House of Lords against a Bill to make machine-breaking a capital offence, and had written to Lord Holland : " Surely, my Lord, however we may rejoice in any improvements in the arts which may be beneficial to mankind, we must not allow mankind to be sacrificed to improvements in mechanism."[1]

In Mary Shelley's story, the monster threatens Frankenstein with the words, " Slave ! Remember that I have power. . . . You are my creator, but I am your master—obey ! "

As often as not, innovations are both welcomed and

[1] Moore's *Life of Byron, anno* 1812.

7

distrusted for the wrong reasons. The Luddite machine-breakers, whose struggle is described in Charlotte Brontë's *Shirley* and in a recent novel, *Inheritance*, by Phyllis Bentley, saw only the immediate menace to their accustomed means of livelihood. Theirs was perhaps a blind and ignorant, certainly a vain and short-lived rebellion. Few of the working-class leaders of the time could see beyond the immediate effect of the new machinery upon their lives. Here and there a man like Robert Owen or John Doherty recognised that the development of machinery was inevitable, and at the same time argued against the economists of the day that the new machinery must be brought under the direction of the working classes themselves. Meanwhile, to the leaders of middle class opinion, the new inventions appeared to open up a prospect of unmixed good in the marvellous material progress that was promised. Lord Macaulay expresses the complacent judgment of his time in his speech on the Reform Bill : " Nowhere does man exercise such a dominion over matter." The Hammonds, in their searching survey of the social history of the period, suggest that the judgment might have been reversed : " Nowhere does matter exercise such a dominion over man."[1]

As the century moved on, strong voices were raised in protest against the mechanisation of man's labour and man's mind. The criticism was often both " generous and confused."[2] Men were coming to see that the material gains that had followed the Industrial Revolution were counter-balanced by human losses—both moral and æsthetic—and Carlyle, Ruskin, Kingsley and Morris were inclined to decry the onward march of machinery and to look back with longing to the Middle Ages. Dr. Clapham sets at the head of his volume *Free Trade*

---

[1] Hammond. *The Town Labourer, p.* 18.
[2] Clapham. *Economic History of Great Britain.* (*Free Trade and Steel.*) p. 482.

and Steel, Ruskin's reference in the 1880 edition of his *Seven Lamps of Architecture* to the " ferruginous temper " which during his lifetime had changed " our Merry England into the Man in the Iron Mask." It is a reversal of the equally extravagant optimism which led Wilberforce at the beginning of the century to speak of " country which Nature seemed to have damned to perpetual sterility " as being " covered by the fruits of human industry and gladdened by the face of man."[1]

We shall attempt in the next chapter to estimate the gains and losses that resulted from the mechanisation of industry ; for the present, I only note that to some minds, even in the midstream of Victorian advance, the new civilisation seemed to mean the spoliation of nature and the degradation of human life and labour.

Some, too, there were, who looked further ahead and prophesied still more spectacular triumphs of machinery for good or ill. Samuel Butler, in letters to the *Christchurch Press* (New Zealand) in 1863, suggested an upshot of mechanical development which he worked out later in the chapters on the Machines in *Erewhon*. In the controversy that led to the final destruction of machinery throughout Erewhon, it was argued that man was becoming a parasite of the machines, an " affectionate machine-ticking aphid," that the machines were rapidly gaining ground and " becoming if not animate, yet something near akin to it." They were even coming to develop a reproductive system by which new machines of wonderful varieties were begotten ; and if not actually alive and conscious, they were, at least, able to indicate their wants and insist on regular feeding and attention at the hands of their slaves.

> " Day by day . . . the machines are gaining ground upon us ; day by day, we are becoming more and more subservient to them ; more men are daily bound down

---

[1] Cited in Hammond, *Rise of Modern Industry*, p. 131.

as slaves to tend them; more men are daily devoting the energies of their whole lives to the development of mechanical life. The upshot is simply a question of time, but that the time will come when the machines will hold the real supremacy over the world and its inhabitants is what no person of a truly philosophic mind can for a moment question.

Our opinion is that war to the death should be instantly proclaimed against them. Every machine of every sort should be destroyed by the well-wisher of his species. Let there be no exceptions made, no quarter shown; let us at once go back to the primeval condition of the race. If it be urged that this is impossible under the present condition of human affairs, this at once proves that the mischief is already done, that our servitude has commenced in real earnest; that we have raised a race of beings whom it is beyond our power to destroy, and that we are not only enslaved, but are absolutely acquiescent in our bondage."[1]

Samuel Butler's ironical warning appears less fantastic to us of to-day who have seen the first mechanical Robot stalk down Piccadilly and who are becoming familiar with talking, singing, writing, calculating and ledgering automata. Lord Lytton, in *The Coming Race*, which anticipated *Erewhon* by a few months, pictured a very different Utopia in which the whole work of society was done by machines which were subservient to man's enjoyment. The machines were in the care of the young people who delighted in their control, and who had at their disposal a mysterious agency called Vril by which they could animate at will the automata that acted as attendants in the house and in the workshop. That prospect, too, appears to us to-day hardly extravagant. New York has recently opened a gigantic power-plant operated without a human being within its walls

---

[1] *The Notebooks of Samuel Butler*, p. 46.

and designed to supply electricity to 300,000 citizens.

But is it Utopia to which this astounding development is hastening us ? This " brave new world " is not regarded by all without alarm. A disquieting prospect is suggested, not only by Aldous Huxley's satire, but by Capek's play, *R.U.R.* (*Rossum's Universal Robots*), and by the German film, *Metropolis*. The play pictures a world of machines made in the likeness of men, the film, a world of men made in the likeness of machines. Both show us, with the vividness of a nightmare—if also with a nightmare's distortion—a vision of what human life may become if the machine civilisation is allowed unchecked to run its course.

In the following chapters, we shall attempt a sober analysis of the trend of events in modern industry, in the light of which it may be possible to judge what measures may be required to safeguard us against the disastrous consequences of a machine civilisation that shall have forgotten man.

CHAPTER II

THE MACHINE CIVILISATION

WHAT is a machine and how does it differ from a tool ? No rigid line of distinction can be drawn between the tool and the machine, any more than between 'domestic manufacture' and the machine industry. The evolution of tools from the prehistoric flint to the 20th century automatic machine, which counts and sorts your coins, delivers your change, and dates, numbers and serves your ticket, is a process marked by continuity, but also by certain well-defined stages.

The primary function of a tool, as the Erewhonian argued who alone was found to defend the machines against extermination, is to serve man as a supplementary detachable limb. In this way, both tools and machines add to the resources of the human body. " Even community of limbs is thus rendered possible . . . for a train is only a seven-leagued boot that five hundred can own at once."[1] A tool, and still more a machine, reinforces the quantity and quality of energy at the disposal of our bodies. The lever, the screw, the pulley, the pump and the wheel adjust the conditions of the work to be done " until the force required to perform it comes within the compass of our muscles."[2] The function of the machine is to transform random and wasteful into disciplined and effective expenditure of energy.[3]

It is usual to say that the tool is a simple machine, and the machine a complex tool, but in fully developed

---

[1] Butler. *Erewhon*, p. 271.
[2] Fournier D'Albe. *Hephaestus*, p. 26.
[3] Chase. *Men and Machines*, p. 271.

machinery there is more than an elaboration of the tool. When Mahatma Gandhi strained his left elbow by constant turning of the spinning wheel, he made use of a pedal for turning the wheel and thus freed his hands for drawing the thread. He denied that he was using a machine. What he probably had in mind was that the motive power was still human. Does, then, the tool become a machine when the motive power is that of an animal, or of natural forces like water and wind ? On this reasoning, as Marx pointed out, a plough would be a tool when driven by man and a machine when driven by oxen ; and one and the same loom a tool when driven by hand and a machine when driven by steam-power. If a distinction is to be drawn between a tool and a machine it may perhaps be first seen in the machine-tool in which the machine contains, handles or grips the tool. A further development is to be seen in the type of machine that characterised the Industrial Revolution. Here the machine is one which " replaces the worker handling a single tool by a mechanism operating simultaneously a number of identical or similar tools and driven by a single motive power, whatever the form of that power may be."[1] The machine is thus labour-saving in a double sense. It at once reinforces and displaces human labour.

In the early days of large-scale industry, horses were largely used as motive-power—hence the survival of the term ' horse-power ' as a measure of mechanical force. Water and wind, and then steam, were substituted as the motive power, until, with the invention of the independent motor mechanism (steam, gas or petrol), it became possible by means of a single motor to drive a number of working machines at once. In fully developed machine production we find three distinct parts—the motor machine (engine or prime mover), the transmitting mechanism (belt or gear), and the mechanical tool or working machine.[2]

---

[1] Marx. *Capital*, p. 396. (Translation E. and C. Paul.)
[2] Marx. *op. cit.*, p. 393.

B

So we come to the machine system, in which subdivision of labour is applied to the working machines, each of which performs a partial operation and supplements the work of the others. The main characteristic of machine production is the 'subdivision of processes' which makes possible the introduction of more and more specialised machines.[1] In what is called 'manufacture' and should be called 'mechano-facture,' we have, then, an organised system of working machines, which are one and all set in motion by the transmitting mechanism from a central power machine.

" In place of the individual machine, we now have a mechanical monster, whose body fills the whole factory, and whose demon power, hidden from our sight at first because of the measured and almost ceremonious character of the movement of his giant limbs, discloses itself at length in the vast and furious whirl of his numberless working organs."[2]

It is the energising of the machine by new forms of power, not as a mere assistance to, but as a substitute for, physical effort, that is the main feature of modern machine industry. " The primary and defining fact about the modern application of science to industrial processes is . . . not the mechanism, but the energy employed."[3]

Ours is the age of power machinery.

Let us now pass in rapid review the main features of the " great industry " and the " great society " which have followed from the application of science to the invention of machinery and the discovery of new forms of power.

(1) In the first place, we may note the " Copernican change "[4] which has taken place in the relations of the worker and the machine, and the *increasing domination of*

[1] Rowe. *Wages in Practice and Theory*, p. 90.
[2] Marx. *Capital*, p. 403.
[3] Henderson. *Economic Consequences of Power Production*, p. 15.
[4] Johnston. *Citizenship in the Industrial World*, p. 31.

machine industry. Although it is true that " machines can produce nothing by themselves"[1] and require to be continually repaired and renewed by human labour, the machine has come to occupy a central and dominating place in modern industry, and the character of industrial work is undergoing rapid transformation. The design, tending and repair of machinery occupies an increasingly large place among industrial occupations.

The generation and transmission of power for the purposes of machine production means that the dynamo is becoming " to our age what the Cathedral was to the Middle Ages."[2] Visitors to Soviet Russia tell us that the machine is taking the place of the *ikon* in schools and public buildings and that representations of machines are displayed as objects of public worship. A friend of mine heard a young Communist boast that the number of factory chimneys was rapidly exceeding the number of church minarets. In the older industrial countries, the worker has not found reason to venerate the factory system to this extent.

(2) The structure and scale of industry have undergone transformation under the influence of machine production. The ' division of labour ' described by Adam Smith as a means of improving manual operations is a development prior to the machine industry—a development that was hastened by the expansion of markets and the increased demand for a number of things of the same kind and of virtually standard size and form. As Marshall pointed out, " the chief effect of the improvement of machinery is to cheapen and make more accurate the work which would anyway have been subdivided."[3]

But the subdivision of labour, by facilitating the *concentration of labour in a single workplace,* made possible the development of the new sources of power. The

[1] Shaw. *Intelligent Woman's Guide to Socialism and Capitalism,* p. 402.
[2] Fox. *The Triumphant Machine,* p. 74.
[3] *Principles of Economics,* Bk. IV, ch. ix., § 3.

factory " embodies in a visible form, the very principle of modern production."[1] In older times carriage-building was the work of largely independent handicrafts ; wheel-wrights, smiths, harness-makers, upholsterers, painters, and so on, each pursued their independent crafts. Assemblage in one workplace makes possible the simultaneous manufacture of numerous vehicles. Similarly, the manufacture of cloth arose through the combination of different crafts under the control of single units of production.

(3) But a further change comes about with the *subdivision of processes* and an increase in mechanical accuracy makes possible the standardisation of products and interchangeability of parts. So we get the beginnings of mass-production with the sewing machine and the bicycle in the eighties of last century and later its application to the manufacture of typewriters, cash registers and the assemblage of motor cars.

(4) A consequence of the reorganisation of industrial methods and a salient feature of the factory system is the *regimentation of labour*. This, which we accept to-day as a matter of course, was a startling innovation in the early days of the Industrial Revolution.[2]

(5) The increasing use of machinery goes along with increasing *Capitalisation*. A larger type of organisation is found to be more economic because of the amount of capital required for installing expensive machinery. A further stage in capitalisation comes about with the growth of the joint stock company, leading to an increasing divorce between the ownership of the capital and the direction and management of industry. A still further development appears in our own time with the colossal concentration of capital in combines—whether amalgama-

---

[1] Mantoux. *The Industrial Revolution in the Eighteenth Century*, p. 26.

[2] See chapter, " The New Discipline," in the Hammonds' *Town Labourer*, and *infra* p. 30.

tions or cartels. Finally, we have the reorganisation of great industrial concerns by large-scale planning of output, works specialisation and marketing policy, which has been described as a " new Industrial Revolution."[1]

(6) One of the earliest consequences of the factory system was the *localisation of industry* and the growth of new towns—the cotton, iron and woollen towns and mining areas. The proportion of the urban to the rural population in this country has steadily risen during the past century, and according to the census of 1931, more than half the population are inhabitants of towns of over 50,000. This process of *urbanisation* is, however, beginning to recede as a result of recent developments in transport and the delivery of cheap electric power to rural districts.

(7) There has been an increasing development of *mass consumption*. The writer (possibly Lord Brougham) who, a hundred years ago, published for the Society for the Diffusion of Useful Knowledge a glowing account of the *Results of Machinery*, boasted that " two centuries ago not one person in a thousand wore stockings ; one century ago not one person in five hundred wore them ; now not one person in a thousand is without them."[2] Machine production has still further multiplied and cheapened the supply of innumerable commodities to the benefit of the mass of the population. None the less, it is in point of distribution that the machine civilisation has most conspicuously failed, and to-day, in spite of our material resources and technical efficiency, we are lamenting the strange conjunction of the embarrassing flow of output which means ' over-production,' and the restricted purchasing power which means ' under-consumption.'

(8) A further accompaniment of the industrial developments of the last century has been the *expansion of population* in both Europe and America. A recent writer

---

[1] See Mr. Walter Meakin's book so entitled.
[2] Hammond. *Rise of Modern Industry*, p. 210.

has pointed out[1] that the population of the North American continent, which was peopled from European stock, is equal to-day to that of all Europe in 1800 ; and at the same time, the population of Europe has trebled. Between 1821 and 1921 the population of England and Wales more than trebled, not by increase in rate of arrival, but by decrease in rate of departure. The birth-rate was approximately steady up to about 1876, since when it has declined, and statisticians anticipate that by the middle of this century our population will stabilise at between forty-eight and forty-nine millions.[2]

(9) Finally, we may note the *expansion of communications* and the development of a world market and a ' world economy.' Railway and motor transport, steamship and oil ship, seaplane, aeroplane and airship, telegraph and telephone, wireless and beam radio have brought the ends of the world together. Travel of persons, transport of goods, transit of news—all are made easy and rapid. Even the stay-at-home is not unaffected. Into his village circle comes the news of the world's events almost as soon as they have taken place (and, by Greenwich time, it may be sooner). Into his village shop come commodities and comestibles from every country of the world—Argentine beef and New Zealand mutton, American oil and Czecho-Slovakian lamp chimneys, Indian tea and Japanese tea-trays.

In older times, a poor harvest in America or Russia or the outbreak of a war in Europe, could hardly affect— even if he knew of it—the ordinary worker at his craft or on his farm. To-day, the security of his livelihood is at once imperilled by the oscillations of the world's exchanges and the fluctuations of the system of international credit. The whole world to-day is a universal market, and a universal whispering gallery, and with the progress of television may become " a universal meeting-place."[3]

---

[1] Garrett, *Ouroboros*, p. 14.
[2] Carr-Saunders and Caradoc Jones. *Social Survey*, pp. 224–226.
[3] Wells. *Work, Wealth and Happiness of Mankind*, p. 153.

CHAPTER III

GAINS AND LOSSES

AN inquiry into the balance of advantages and disadvantages following from the multiplication of machinery
reveals the superficiality of the sweeping generalisations
which are offered on the one side or the other.   Nor is it
possible to tabulate a neat list of gains which can be set
out under separate heads like the credit side of a balance
sheet with a neat list of losses over against them on the
debit side.   The business of ethical accountancy is not so
easily susceptible of neat arrangement.   An item which
at first appears to be an unmixed evil or an unmixed good,
turns out on closer examination to be less easy to place or
to appraise.   We find ourselves constantly needing to
distinguish and subdivide and disentangle, and even then
the threads of good and evil are inextricably interwoven.
Moreover, to return to the figure of the balance sheet, it
is not enough to look at the profit or loss account for the
preceding year alone—what is needed is a comparative
statement by which each of the items as well as the totals
can be judged in relation to a period of years.   From this
standpoint it would be necessary to ask, first, how the
machine civilisation compares in various points of importance to mankind with earlier conditions of life and
labour, and second, in what respects we have advanced or
receded during the actual period of machine industry.   It
is, for example, important to recognise that there are
conditions incidental to the early stages of machine
industry in this country which are not essential to it and
which have largely disappeared in later stages.   The
Hammonds are careful to point out that the displacement
of hand labour by machinery was not the chief cause

either of the distress of the period of which they are treating in the *Town Labourer* (1760–1832), or of the revolt of the workers. That cause they assign to the new power of capital, which exploited not only machinery but human life.

" The real conflict of the time is the struggle of the various classes, some working in factories, some working in their own homes, to maintain a standard of life. The struggle is not so much against machinery as against the power behind machinery, the power of capital. . . . The miner who had never been a domestic worker, and the handloom weaver who remained a domestic worker, were just as sensible of this power as the spinner who went into the factory to watch a machine do the work that had been done in the cottage. and the shearman who tried unavailingly to keep out of the gig-mill."[1]

The same point is brought home to us if we recall that Tom Hood's *Song of the Shirt*, with its picture of the domestic seamstress, appeared in *Punch* in 1843, and that Mrs. Browning's *Cry of the Children*, with its picture of the child worker in the factories, was published in the following year. " In the domestic system of manufacture," says M. Mantoux, " children were exploited as a matter of course."[2]

The exploitation of children in the East to-day is equally evident in handwork and machine work. In the Cairo silk-winding and hand rug-making shops may be seen " tiny children of five and a half years and upwards working like rapid machines . . . with all expression of childhood gone from their faces,"[3] while in the neighbouring cigarette and tobacco factories children are working amid imperfectly guarded machinery. Here the worst abuses are being remedied by the Egyptian Government as a consequence of Dame Adelaide Anderson's

[1] *The Town Labourer*, pp. 15–16.   [2] *op. cit.*, p. 422.
[3] Wells. *Work, Wealth and Happiness of Mankind*, p. 256.

report in the *Review* of the International Labour Office. It is significant that among the worst and last-surviving of our own " sweated " industries, now brought under the Trade Board system, was that of cheap ready-made clothing in the homes and small workshops of East London.

We must not, then, attribute to machinery or the machine system the responsibility for the evils of industrialism. Here, as so often, it is only too easy to commit the fallacy of reasoning *post hoc ergo propter hoc*, a fallacy which misleads not only those who argue that machinery is responsible for all the evils of industrialism but also those who argue that machinery is responsible for all its benefits. That those benefits are immense, whatever the precise part that machinery has played, and without wishing to exaggerate its importance in comparison with other factors, it is impossible to deny.

" The artisan or mechanic and his family, and to a lesser degree the unskilled labourer and his family, are to-day enjoying a definitely higher standard of life than the corresponding sections of the population at any previous period in the world's history . . . The homes in which these wage earners and their families live, even taking into account the shocking conditions still prevailing in many places, are more soundly constructed, more commodious and convenient, more abundantly and more comfortably furnished, with immensely better sanitation, and placed amid surroundings superior in respect of hygiene and amenity to anything usual in any previous century. These families, husband, wife and children, are far better fed than their forebears of any previous generation. They have more leisure after their work, and greater opportunity of making good use of their leisure. . . . The reward which is the result of their work is, taking the manual-working class as a whole, greater than ever before ; and what is now almost always a money wage commands a vastly widened range of commodities and services effectively brought within their reach, according to their choice : and in the aggregate an increased amount of such commodities and services, in comparison with what fell to the lot of the manual workers when they were for the most part independent producers."[1]

" The little children of 1931, class for class, are better grown, better looking, more scientifically fed and clothed, than children have ever been before, and their minds develop more freely."[2]

" Within a decade of the Armistice not only the world as a whole, but even belligerent Europe, had a substantially higher standard of life than in 1913."[3]

There is no reason, it would seem, to lament with Mr. Penty the passing of the ' good old days ' to which he looks back in his *Old Worlds for New*. Whatever good and pleasant features were to be found in the life and labour of mediæval Europe, there were countervailing evils that should deter anyone from wishing, even if it were possible, for a restoration of the old ways. The Italian historian Ferrero is said to have recommended anyone who has romantic yearnings after the good old times " to spend one night in what our forefathers called a bed."[4] And Prof. J. B. S. Haldane remarks in *Daedalus* : " Bad as our urban conditions often are, there is not a slum in the country which has a third of the infantile death-rate of the royal family in the Middle Ages."[5]

But let us turn from the general conditions of living in which we may trace so imposing an advance, to the particular conditions of work, in respect of which the introduction of machinery has had a most easily discernible and direct influence.

---

[1] Sidney and Beatrice Webb, in a contribution to an American publication, *Whither Mankind ?* p. 137.
[2] Wells. *Work, Wealth and Happiness of Mankind*, p. 555.
[3] Salter. *Recovery*, p. 24.
[4] Zimmern. *Nationality and Government*, p. 150.
[5] p. 54.

(1) And, first, what about *toil*, meaning heavy and exhausting labour ? Here there is a good deal to be said for the view that the use of machinery has " taken the backache out of industry." And lest anyone should suppose that this merely means the elimination of healthy muscular exercise, let us look at what toil actually meant to the pre-industrial worker. Take the work of the carpenter. Before the days of steam mills for sawing, planing and moulding, carpenters suffered fatigue and strain from sheer toil which made them prematurely old. " All but skilled men," says Marshall, " were compelled to spend a great part of their time with the jackplane, and this brought on heart disease, making them as a rule old men by the time they were forty." And he quotes Adam Smith's description of the way in which workers would over-work themselves and ruin their health and constitution in a few years.

" A carpenter in London and in some places is not supposed to last in his utmost vigour above eight years. . . . Almost every class of artificer is subject to some particular infirmity occasioned by excessive application to their peculiar species of work."[1] ·

Take a further account of weaving in Witney, in 1767, that comes to us from Arthur Young's *Southern Tour*.

" There are about 500 weavers in the town. . . . Journeymen, in general, on an average, earn from 10s. to 12s. a week, all the year round . . . but they work from 4 to 8, and in winter by candle light."[2]

Even to-day, in the non-industrial parts of China, you find conditions of work that are not less exhausting than the conditions of the Shanghai factories—terrible as those are.

An American observer, writing in 1924, says :—

" Nearly all the lumber used in China is hand-sawn,

[1] Marshall. *Economics of Industry*, p. 148.
[2] For the reference I am indebted to Dr. Alfred Plummer.

and the sawyers are exhausted early. Physicians agree that carrying coolies rarely live beyond forty-five or fifty years. The term of a chair-bearer is eight years, of a rickshaw runner four years, for the rest of his life he is an invalid."[1]

A Chinese contributor to the volume *Whither Mankind?* remarks that in Japan to-day in the industrial centres of Yokohama and Tokio the rickshaw coolie is rapidly disappearing. And his disappearance has been brought about not by humanitarianism, but " by the advent of the ' one-yen-within-the-city ' Ford car."[2]

At many points, then, we must admit that human toil has been appreciably diminished by the increased use of machinery, and that a good deal more human toil and drudgery—both manual and clerical—might be relieved if human life were not considered cheaper than the installation of machinery. It is said that in Lisbon (even in 1925) the work of coaling steamships (for which machinery was available on the spot) was performed by cheap female labour. There is work still done to-day in England—in charging boilerhouse furnaces or the ovens of a hand labour coking plant, that is exhausting, degrading and monotonous. In a coal mine without modern equipment—and there are many such—there is the ' tramming ' of tubs from the coal face to the haulage road, and the pushing and pulling of tubs on and off the cages.

Contrast this picture—a little overdrawn no doubt, but substantially accurate—of modernised methods in the Ruhr coalfields.

" The mechanics or other attendants who control a modern boiler house, free from smoke, dirt and fumes, the men who operate the electrical machines by which a modern coking plant is entirely operated, the pithead

---

[1] *Compare* the 18th century *Running Footman*, described in John Owen's novel of that name.

[2] p. 33.

worker who sits at a switchboard and controls the automatic devices which move the tubs from the cage, empty the coal on to the screens, and return the tubs to the cage, the engineer who controls the gigantic machines which scoop up 200 tons of brown coal an hour, the men who operate the various kinds of conveyors, which have abolished an immense amount of pushing and lifting, are all using intelligence and skill. Their work is comparatively clean. They finish the day fresh enough, physically and mentally, to foster interests apart from their employment. They have a new status in industry, which was never attainable by the old-type labourers, whose work has been transformed by the new machines."[1]

There are other considerations that require to be taken into account, but it is that kind of contrast which explains the enthusiasm of the advocates of machinery, enthusiasm that leads one of them to the extravagant but understandable exclamation that 1769—the year of Watt's first ' fire-machine '—was " the great milestone of mankind," because on that day " man ceased to be a beast of burden and was given his first chance to become a human being."[2]

If we set over against this panegyric the famous passage on machinery in John Stuart Mill's *Principles of Political Economy*, we must remember that it was written in 1848.

" Hitherto it is questionable if all the inventions yet made have lightened the day's toil of any human being. They have enabled a greater population to live the same life of drudgery and imprisonment, and an increased number of manufacturers and others to make fortunes. They have increased the comforts of the middle classes. But they have not yet begun to effect those great changes in human destiny, which it is in their nature to

[1] Meakin. *The New Industrial Revolution*, p. 241.
[2] Van Loon in *Whither Mankind?* p. 43.

accomplish. Only when, in addition to just institutions, the increase of mankind shall be under the deliberate guidance of judicious foresight, can the conquests made from the powers of nature by the intellect and energy of scientific discoverers become the common property of the species, and the means of improving and elevating the universal lot."[1]

Professor J. H. Clapham, who expressly draws attention to the date when this was written, adds a comment on the changes that Mill might have recorded had he revised his judgment when he published his later editions in the ' eighties.'

" Some heavy, even murderous jobs had been killed or nearly killed by machinery since he first wrote. There were few ' bottom-sawyers ' left ; few, if any, carpenters worked out in fifteen years by handling the great jackplane. The sewing machine must have lightened an incalculable number of days' toil. It was easier to mind a completely self-acting mule than to push about the carriage of the old hand-mule. The power-loom shed was noisy, and its looms had been speeded up ; but work in it was certainly lighter, day for day, than the bowed endless insanitary monotony of that lower grade hand-loom weaving of the ' thirties ' and ' forties ' which alone had been completely superseded. Scything is a noble art ; but it cannot be argued that a full day's scything is lighter than a full day's management of a reaper ; nor that a day in an un-mechanised copper or lead mine is lighter than one in a fully equipped colliery.

" Yet if mechanical invention was killing off some heavy jobs, it had made and was making others— stoking and coal-trimming in a gale, or in the Red Sea ; puddling, and all the scores of laborious and often dangerous tasks in gas works, chemical works and

---

[1] Bk. IV, ch. vi, § 2.

engineering shops. An hour's work in the caissons, or on the cantilevers of the Forth Bridge may well be called heavier than one put in under Rennie on Waterloo Bridge. So the enumeration might go on, but no balance could ever be struck. For it is not even quite certain that twelve and a half hours' work, paced by the ' wheels of iron ' in the early cotton mills, was heavier for the child than twelve and a half hours of many different drudgeries to which he might have been assigned before the inventions."[1]

(2) To-day it is safe to say that toil, in the sense of laborious and exhausting work, is largely eliminated by the use of machinery. But what are we to say of *monotony*? It is frequently asserted that work is more monotonous and tedious to-day because of the increase in repetitive process jobs in mass-production. Yet it is important to remember, first, that machinery has eliminated many monotonous forms of hand labour, and second, that new machinery is increasingly taking over the more monotonous forms of repetition machine work. Marshall pointed out the extent to which machinery in weaving relieved the monotony of the earlier handweaving.

" Nothing could be more monotonous than the occupation of a weaver of plain stuffs in the old time. But now one woman will manage four or more looms, each of which does many times as much work in the course of the day as the handloom did, and her work is much less monotonous and calls for much more judgment than his did. So that for every hundred yards of cloth that are woven, the purely monotonous work done by human beings is probably not one-twentieth part of what it was."[2]

If we think of sewing before the invention of the sewing-machine, of sawing before the invention of the

---

[1] Clapham. *Economic History of Modern Britain* (1850–1886), p. 446.
[2] *Economics of Industry*, Bk. IV, ch. ix., § 3.

steam-saw, of the many monotonous and repetitive operations in wrapping and folding, or cigarette-rolling by hand, and of the clerical occupations which have been replaced by the printing press, the typewriter and the adding-machine, we realise that while new forms of repetition work have come in, there are as many more that have gone out. Moreover, it is precisely the more monotonous and repetitive machine processes that are capable of being further mechanised and handed over to more and more automatic machinery. An operation that we call mechanical is *ipso facto* capable of mechanisation, and we consequently arrive at the paradoxical conclusion of M. de Man that " the best way of de-mechanising work is to hand it over to a machine."[1]

(3) But if we may expect a balance of advantage in the elimination by machinery of toilsome and monotonous work, we confront a more obstinate difficulty when we consider the element of *nervous tension*. It is generally agreed that the sense of strain, consequent in part on ' speeding-up ' and in part on the factor of noise and clatter, is greatly increased by machinery and machine methods of production.

George Bourne, writing in 1923 of the difference between work to-day and work as he knew it in the period from 1884 to 1891, says :—

> " In those days a man's work, though more laborious to his muscles, was not nearly so exhausting yet tedious as machinery and ' speeding-up ' have since made it for his mind and temper. ' Eight hours ' to-day is less interesting and probably more toilsome[2] than ' twelve hours ' then.[3]

> " In modern conditions work is nothing like so tolerable as it was say thirty years ago ; partly because

---

[1] *Joy in Work*, p. 112 (for a fuller discussion of monotony see Chapter VII).

[2] *sic :* ' irksome ' would be the better word. (cf. *infra*, p. 79.)

[3] *The Wheelwright's Shop*, p. 16. (By George Bourne=Sturt.)

there is more hurry in it, but largely because machinery has separated employers from employed and has robbed the latter of the sustaining delights which materials used to afford them. Work is less and less pleasant to do—unless perhaps, for the engineer or the electrician."[1]

Here several factors are noted, some of them more directly attributable to the nature of machine work and others dependent on extraneous conditions. A combination of factors conducing to nervous strain is also suggested by Mr. Pound in *The Iron Man*:

"There develops among the workers in highly automatised plants a chronic dissatisfaction, which cannot be explained without reference to nerves. It seems to be proof against high wages and good conditions. Welfare work, bonuses, shop councils, even profit-sharing do not drive it out. So pervasive is this malady that it might be described as a work-neurosis. Clatter and haste are contributing factors; so also are indoor confinement, monotony of task, distance from the real boss, repression of personality, strict regimentation of effort, and the scant opportunity afforded for the play of the craftsman instinct, the joy in production."[2]

There are four main sources of nervous strain under which the factors mentioned in these extracts may be grouped.

(a) There is the divorce of man from the soil and from 'natural' conditions of life and work. Man's body and mind were first developed in contact with earth and open country, and in spite of his astonishing capacity for adaptation it is doubtful if city life and indoor work can ever satisfy him even though it may not irk him consciously. It is estimated that in England "about three out of every four occupied persons follow an indoor

[1] *The Wheelwright's Shop*, p. 202.   [2] p. 165.

C

calling."[1]   It is significant that the Greek disparagement of the work of the artisan as vulgar or banal (βαναυσικόν) was not merely based on the fact that it left a man without sufficient leisure for ' the good life,' but on the fact that it meant a stuffy indoor occupation, and often sedentary, and that this was considered enervating alike to body and to mind.[2]   The pathetic attempt of the city worker to find some pale satisfaction in a suburban garden or allotment and of the city youth or girl to escape into the countryside by week-end ' hiking ' bears witness to a deep-rooted disposition that will not be denied.

(b) The conditions of modern work offend in other ways against the natural make-up of man.   His powers were evolved for intermittent activity ' by fits and starts ' rather than for regular and uniform spells and rates of working.[3]   It was here that the ' new discipline ' of the factory system was felt to be most unnatural and obnoxious.   The regularity of hours, the constant drive and pressure, and the penalties for petty misdemeanours like whistling or moving about,[4] replaced a mode of life and work that may not have meant more leisure but was at least more ' leisurely ' and allowed for some degree of freedom to ' knock off ' when one felt inclined.   And the difference between ' knocking off ' and ' clocking off ' is a substantial one.   M. Mantoux says of the domestic worker :—

> " Even though at home he had to work long hours to make up for the lowness of his wages, yet he could begin and stop at will, and without regular hours.   He could divide up the work as he chose, come and go,

[1] Carr-Saunders and Jones. *Social Survey*, p. 53.
[2] Xenophon. *Œconomicus*, iv, 3.
[3] Wallas. *Social Heritage*, p. 28. " Civilised man, therefore, when he digs potatoes, or adds up figures, as his regular daily occupation, is using continuously, under the direction of self-conscious will, powers which were evolved for intermittent use under the direction of impulse ; and he suffers, in consequence, daily fatigue, and at longer intervals severe nervous reaction."
[4] Hammond. *Town Labourer*, p. 20-1.

rest for a moment, and even, if he chose, be idle for days together."[1]

" He had some say in his own life "[2] and sometimes combined farming with weaving or spinning. The factory system involving of necessity a regular and uniform discipline and organisation, entails an inevitable ' baulking '[3] of man's natural dispositions which becomes more serious with the increase of mechanisation and regimentation in the large-scale industrial concern.

It is, however, not only the arrangement and ordering of a man's working life that is liable to set up a nervous strain, but the character of the work itself on which he is engaged. If it does not evoke any interest in the doing of it, it is bound to be done listlessly. We shall deal later[4] with the question how far the intrinsic interest of craftmanship has been lost in modern industry and how far new forms of interest and skill, as well as new incentives to work, are growing up. Meanwhile, it must be admitted that the conditions of modern industry are not only failing for many workers to satisfy their dispositions, but are often felt to be ' against the grain.'

(c) A further source of nervous strain that is more particularly attributable to the multiplication of machinery is to be found in the increasing element of speed and clatter. The domination of the worker and of his natural working ' tempo ' by the externally imposed rhythm of power-driven machinery is a point to which we shall return,[5] but it must be noted here as a factor in setting up a condition of nervous strain.

Noise and clatter, as well as bustle, are liable, in spite of man's capacity for adaptation, to set up at least unconsciously a certain degree of nervous irritation, which,

---

[1] *op. cit.*, p. 419.
[2] Hammond. *Skilled Labourer*, p. 3.
[3] Wallas. *Great Society*, ch. 4.
[4] See Chapters V and X.   [5] See Chapter VIII.

though he may not know the cause, will make him restless, dissatisfied, and less capable of dealing patiently with other disturbances of his mental poise in the home or in his relations with his fellows.[1]

(d) A fourth factor in occasioning nervous strain is to be seen in the personal and social relationships or lack of relationships in large-scale industry. It is true that the older types of organisation have been unduly glorified, and that there is evidence of frequent friction in the relations of masters and journeymen in mediæval industry.[2] But though it may be fanciful to speak regretfully of the change by which a ' master ' ceased to mean a master of his craft and came to mean a master of others[3] there was at least a possibility in the pre-industrial association between employer and employed of an intimate and even friendly co-operation. This became less easy of attainment under the factory system and still less so with the further separation of ownership and work under the Joint Stock Company system and the increasing scale of industrial organisation, which reaches even wider limits in the modern industrial combine.

Here, too, the demand for more rigid regimentation of the industrial personnel has introduced an element not only of distance between the individual operative and the ultimate and invisible management, but of subordination to the arbitrary rule of immediately superior foremen who possess the power of dismissal or promotion without the prestige, however superstitiously regarded, attaching to the older master-owner.

---

[1] cf. p. 68 *infra*.
[2] See Hammond. *Rise of Modern Industry*, p. 206 (quoting Unwin).
[3] *op. cit.*, p. 249 (quoting G. K. Chesterton).

CHAPTER IV

(4) ONE of the most frequent indictments of mechanical civilisation is that it makes for *standardisation*. This is a generalisation that requires more careful examination. In particular, we need to distinguish between different kinds of standardisation.[1]

(a) In the technical sense of the term, ' standardisation ' means the use of standard units of measurement or the standard production of interchangeable parts which facilitates the process of mass-production. Along with ' simplification,' or the attempt to reduce the number of sizes and varieties in the products of manufacture, it conduces to efficiency and accuracy in production and the elimination of waste and confusion. Neither standardisation nor simplification in this sense can be said to imperil the individuality of the consumer. I cannot complain that my individuality is threatened by the fact that I have 384 varieties of spade to choose from in place of 4,460 in the past, or that I have to make my choice between 25 varieties of blackboard slate in place of 251.[2]

(b) Another and a consequent meaning of standardisation is the fact that mass-production methods put upon the markets an enormous quantity of standard commodities from matchboxes to motor-cars. Here again the range of choice is far from being restricted, as one may see by glancing through any sales catalogue, and the cheapening of price of the articles produced enables a

---

[1] See Chase. *Men and Machines*, ch. 15.
[2] See p. 160 *infra*.

far greater number of persons to exercise any choice at all. For it must be remembered that consumption in pre-industrial times and countries is standardised for the mass of people *at a low level* by bare necessity. To-day the effect of modern industry is enormously to " increase the variety of choice, in food, clothing, in housing and the occupations of leisure."[1] The real trouble is not so much the standardisation of useful commodities as the multiplication of useless ones—the production in bewildering variety of gadgets and gewgaws on which we waste alike our money, our attention and our time. It is *vulgarisation* rather than standardisation that is the evil to be deplored. And this is to be seen in two ways. There is, on the one hand, an emphasis on quantity rather than quality, and on the other hand an emphasis on changing fashion rather than on durability. The multiplication of the ' cheap and nasty ' is an old complaint against machine production. Quality of material, of form, and of workmanship is often sacrificed to quantity and speed of output. And the very capacity of the machine to disgorge prodigious quantities of whatever is required puts a premium on careless and wasteful use of what can be so easily replaced. Moreover, fashion is more and more shortlived, and when changes of fashion are fast and frequent there is scant inducement to use durable materials or to make things sound and strong enough to last, especially when economic interests require a constant forcing of the market.

(c) A third sense of standardisation is the standardisation of taste, opinion and behaviour. Here again we may first point out that the most rigidly standardised societies are the most primitive and backward, and that the static condition of such societies as well as of civilisations like that of the old Chinese Empire is due to their isolation. Machinery, by promoting ease of communication, makes for the spread of ideas, and for intellectual

[1] Delisle Burns. *Leisure in the Modern World*, p. 172.

and spiritual cross-fertilisation. But while the mechanical means of communication help in this way to promote variety, the mechanical multiplication of 'records' tends to promote uniformity. The printing press, the wireless, the gramophone and the film reduplicate vast quantities of identical material. Here as in the provision of food and clothing, the variety of types is innumerable, so that cheap books, newspapers and magazines, cheap cinema seats and radio sets and gramophone records put at the disposal of the mass of people, even in remote country villages, a variety of information and entertainment of unprecedented profusion and confusion.

Here, too, we find vulgarisation a greater danger than standardisation. The characteristic of our time is not so much a standardised set of opinions and beliefs, as a bewildering flux of conflicting opinions and beliefs, in which the older standards are discredited. Men ask themselves whether, having 'gone off the gold standard' of an older moral code, they will be able to 'peg' moral conduct in the future to any stable standard of moral values. The same confusion, arising from a revolt from older orthodoxies, without any agreement upon new standards in their place, is to be seen in the sphere of art.

But, though mechanical aids to education and entertainment expand the range of man's interest and enjoyment if only of the secondhand and the second rate, they are undoubtedly liable to be exploited, whether by vested interests or governments, for the purpose of standardised propaganda and mass-suggestion.

(5) A mechanical civilisation is often held to mean a *materialistic* civilisation. How far is this true ? Materialism, in the sense here implied, means a preoccupation with the material conditions of living and especially with monetary and quantitative standards, to the detriment or exclusion of moral, æsthetic or spiritual values. We have seen that the last century has witnessed an un-

exampled improvement in the standard of life for the mass of people in Western Europe and the United States of America. In so far as this means relief from the pressure of material want and increase of leisure it should have the effect of liberating men's minds for wider interests and enjoyments. The expansion of educational facilities and of the means of communication contributes to the same end. And on the whole we must recognise a widespread cultural improvement among industrial peoples which marks a real advantage over pre-industrial periods and areas. It is at least doubtful if the Middle Ages, to which the opponents of machinery have cast back a longing glance, represent a more spiritual civilisation than that of our own time; and the Age of Faith would be more accurately termed the Age of Superstition.

Again, a Chinese contributor to the volume *Whither Mankind?* emphatically insists that the term 'materialistic civilisation' is far more appropriate to the pre-industrial civilisations of the East than to the industrial civilisations of the West.

> "Do we seriously believe" (he asks) "that there can be any spiritual life left in those poor human beasts of burden who run and toil and sweat under that peculiar bondage of slavery which knows neither the minimum wage nor any limit of working hours?"[1]

M. Henri de Man has reminded us that "in a retrospect of earlier years, we have no right to identify the conditions of the masses with that of a small and culturally dominant stratum," and that the only fair comparison is "between persons who belong to kindred social strata in the respective epochs." And he points out that the reports he has obtained from machine workers show "that they become less and less inclined to show hostility to machinery, in proportion as they attain a higher level of occupational and general culture, in proportion as

---

[1] Mr. Hu Shi, in *Whither Mankind?* p. 29.

their social needs and intellectual standards are higher."

"Were it true," he continues, "as is currently believed by intellectuals, that spiritualised ideals are incompatible with mechanised labour, it would be especially among the more intelligent and socially more exacting upper strata of the working-class (those to which the writers of the reports belong), that we should find the most declared hostility towards machine and factory production. Yet, the very reverse of this is true."[1]

It is arguable that the widespread use of the terms 'materialism' and 'materialistic' betokens a stage of consciousness that has already envisaged spiritual values, and that we should not talk so freely about 'materialistic civilisation' if we were solely preoccupied with material things. Even the Materialistic Conception of History can be shown to point beyond itself. For if the ideology of a particular period is held to reflect the current economic and technical conditions of production, the materialistic ideology itself may be regarded as the temporary and limited reflection of an economic age that is already passing. Materialism may indeed be said to be already old-fashioned and that is why it is so dogmatically held by its remaining adherents, for a dogma has been well defined as "a truth of which men have forgotten that it ever had a history and are determined that it shall have none in the future."

What is characteristic of our time is an increasing uncertainty and unrest which is the sign of a civilisation that has lost its bearings. The rapidity with which the changes due to machinery have come upon us has not allowed us time to ask in what direction we want to go, and we therefore try now this, now that direction, with a speed of movement and also of alteration and reversal which machinery itself makes possible. But the resulting

[1] *Joy in Work*, pp. 92–94.

temper, far from being either uniform and standardised or mechanical and materialistic, is a profoundly disturbing spiritual unrest and dissatisfaction.

All that we have said on the advantages and disadvantages that have followed from the advance of mechanical inventions suggests that the evils which we associate with machinery and machine production are mainly due either to the use to which they are put, or the failure to decide what uses they are best worth putting to. The evils of the first phase of the Industrial Revolution have been shewn to follow not from the introduction of machinery itself but from the conditions under which it was developed and the uses to which it was primarily directed. The Hammonds have drawn attention to the domination of the motive of " rapid and unthinking profit "[1] in the exploitation of the new machinery and the new power. The new masters " valued machinery as a means, not to a larger or richer life for the workers, but to greater and quicker profits for their enterprise."[2]

" Everything turned to profit. The towns had their profitable dirt, their profitable smoke, their profitable slums, their profitable disorder, their profitable ignorance, their profitable despair. The curse of Midas was on this society."[3]

The hideous defilement of nature and the callous treatment of man in the early days of the Industrial Revolution argue a thoughtlessness and brutality which were already rampant in a new employing class that had been reared in the depressed conditions of a pre-industrial society. The emancipated slave may make a tyrannical task master, and it is not machinery but greed for gain that must be held responsible for the spoliation of the mining valleys and the ugly and planless building of the

---

[1] *Rise of Modern Industry*, p. 256.
[2] *The Skilled Labourer*, p. 5.
[3] *Rise of Modern Industry*, p. 232.

new manufacturing towns with their " dark Satanic mills." It is only in our own time that men are slowly beginning to take thought—often too late—about town planning and design and smoke abatement and the preservation of the countryside. And if our machine civilisation is accompanied by a " slick, pitiful commonplace vulgarity,"[1] this is not only no new disease, but is happily offset by the growth of a new social and æsthetic conscience that is increasingly concerned about the conditions under which men labour, to the end that their work may be better adapted to the workers' needs and that the products of work may be made at once more beautiful and useful.

The question, then, that remains at the close of our examination of the balance sheet of gains and losses is the question what use we shall make of the vast resources that scientific invention and mechanical production have put at our disposal. Meanwhile, we shall not be saved either by the worship of machinery or by denunciation of it, and we cannot too often remind ourselves that there are other false gods more deadly than Vulcan whose worship is around us, and that our worst evils may come from the worship of Mammon and of Mars.

[1] R. M. Fox. *The Triumphant Machine*, p. 76.

CHAPTER V

NEW SKILLS FOR OLD

THERE are few expressions in industry of more baffling vagueness and uncertainty of definition than the term ' *skill* ' or the reference to ' *skilled* ' and ' *unskilled* ' labour. When it is alleged that skill is being supplanted by machinery, or that skilled labour is decreasing in comparison with unskilled or semi-skilled, it is not only important to examine the facts of the situation to know precisely what is happening but also to arrive at some clearer definition of the meaning of skill and of the various kinds and degrees of skill.

As a general definition we may take that which is proposed by Professor T. H. Pear—" The ability to do a relatively complicated thing easily and well."[1] This is sufficiently wide to include intellectual as well as manual performances, though elsewhere Dr. Pear himself tends to confine the term ' skill ' to manual dexterities and to equate it with what he calls ' muscular knowledge.' For the purpose of classifying occupations as relatively skilled or unskilled, it would appear to be impossible to limit the term ' skilled ' to manual work and not to apply it to intellectual, administrative and clerical work. The terms ' mental ' and ' manual ' work are also exceedingly misleading and the distinction between ' workers by brain ' and ' workers by hand ' more often than not fallacious. Most forms of ' handwork ' involve a fine co-ordination between brain and hand and many forms of ' brain-work ' are mechanical and unexacting. There are

---

[1] Pear. *Skill in Work and Play*, pp. 20–21. See also Long and Pear. *Industrial Health Research Board, Report 64.*

many instances of class distinction and class prejudice, especially within what is known as the ' working class,' which may be shewn to be most ridiculously unfounded on closer examination of the facts.

Taking the term ' skill ' in general to apply to any form of ability to do a more or less complicated performance, we may attempt to distinguish the factors which go to its development before examining the various kinds and grades of skilled performance. Skill is dependent upon two main factors, one of which is innate and the other acquired, namely, capacity and trained practice. The former will include both the degree of general intelligence (for which the symbol g is used) which it is attempted to discover and assess by means of ' intelligence ' tests, and the degree of specific aptitude (for which the symbol s is used) for this or that accomplishment, which it is attempted to discover and assess by means of ' special ability ' tests. But neither the capacity known as intelligence nor the capacities or aptitudes for special kinds of performance themselves constitute more than the raw material of skill or skills. The second factor of trained practice is necessary to transform capacity into ability. I say ' trained practice ' for it is obvious that mere habitual practice does not necessarily make for skilful performance. Although we are accustomed to say that ' practice makes perfect,' this, like most proverbs, records only a half-truth. Repeated exercise makes for ease and usually, no doubt, for improved performance, but it may only serve to confirm initial errors and so consolidate and stereotype an imperfect performance. The habitual performance is the one most often repeated and consequently easiest, but skill consists in the elimination of the less efficient movements, however frequently performed before, and the selection of those which are best adapted to the purpose of the work in hand. Habit, again, relaxes attention, but for the sake of proficiency it may be desirable to restore attention in order that we may reach a skilled accomplishment, and not a merely perfunctory and mediocre performance.

Skill, then, involves training as well as practice, and is usually marked by an " integration of well-adjusted performances."[1] But a further distinction arises here between what may be called ' all-round ' and specialised skill. Specialised training may make for a certain high degree of proficiency in a relatively limited series of operations, but the skill so developed will not be readily transferable. The classification of ' skilled ' and ' un-skilled ' workers has often turned upon the period of training or apprenticeship to a particular occupation or set of operations. But through defect either of aptitude or methods of training the worker classed as ' skilled ' may be relatively unskilled. On the other hand, a worker who is classified as ' unskilled ' because he has not been trained to any specialised craft or occupation, may have acquired in the course of a varied experience a ' handiness ' and versatility that must be allowed to be a high degree of skill.[2]

We need, then, to include under the term ' skilled performance ' a number of different kinds of accomplishment which may be classified as follows :—

(a) Muscular dexterity—involving repeated practice ranging from mere muscular habituation to " the integration of well-adjusted performance " which may be called ' muscular knowledge ' or manipulative ' knack.'

(b) Artistic craftsmanship—involving originality in designing, and artistry in execution.

(c) Technical expertness—involving experience and knowledge of tools or machines and mechanical processes.

(d) ' All round ' adaptability or versatility,—involving varied experience and ingenuity in dealing with changing situations.

---

[1] Pear. *Fitness for Work*, p. 23.

[2] Pear and Long. *Industrial Health Research Board Report*, No 64, p. 5.

(e) Inventive ability—involving originality in devising new processes, designing new machinery, and adjusting new ideas to existing practice.

(f) Trained judgment and administrative ability—involving insight and foresight, experience of men and affairs, 'business sense,' and ability to plan and direct.

We may now examine how far these various forms of skill are advancing or receding under the conditions of mechanical industry. At first sight, it would appear that we must acknowledge a position of unquestioned and unqualified loss in point of manual dexterity and craftsmanship. And certainly there are crafts that have been displaced, with the result that a great part of the skill that has been handed down in them has disappeared or is disappearing. This is the aspect of the situation that looms up in the minds of those who look back to the small village crafts, one of which is so vividly and memorably depicted in George Bourne's *The Wheelwright's Shop*. What he most deeply laments in his book is the loss of that intimacy with materials and tools which the old craftsman enjoyed.

" No higher wage, no income, will buy for men that satisfaction which of old—until machinery made drudges of them—streamed into their muscles all day long from close contact with iron, timber, clay, wind and wave, horse-strength. It tingled up in the niceties of touch, sight, scent. The very ears unawares received it, as when the plane went singing over the wood, or the exact chisel went tapping in (under the mallet) to the hard ash with gentle sound. But these intimacies are over. Although they have so much more leisure, men can now taste little solace in life, of the sort that skilled hand-work used to yield to them . . . In what was once the wheelwright's shop, where Englishmen grew friendly with the grain of timber and with sharp tool, nowadays untrained youths wait upon machines, hardly knowing oak from ash or caring for the qualities of either."[1]

It may be that nothing in machine work quite takes the place of this loving acquaintance with the feel of timber and of tools (though there are workers in steel and at machines who speak with no less enthusiasm), but the question still remains for how many workers in former times this joy was possible. Those who have studied the history of the mediæval craftsman remind us of other considerations.

" In the heyday of the mediæval guild, there were always, even in the most artistic cities, far more manual workers outside the favoured circle of masters, journey-men and apprentices, than within it. . . . What a multitude of labourers quarried the stones, dragged and carried the stones and lifted the stones of the cathedral walls on which half a dozen skilled and artistic masons carved gargoyles ! "[2]

In our own time it is further to be remembered that some of the worst conditions surviving in industry are to be found in the production of hand-made goods. Take this statement :—

" It is the workers who turn out beautiful hand-worked lace and delicate garments whose working conditions are most appalling, even in advanced in-dustrial countries. And let every social reformer who sentimentally raves over the superior beauty of the craftsmanship of hand-production in Oriental rugs remember that the work was being done in the year 1921 in Persia, by children of five or six years of age employed in appalling conditions for twelve or fourteen hours per day."[3]

Moreover we are liable to assume from the examples of

<hr>

[1] *The Wheelwright's Shop*, p. 202.
[2] S. and B. Webb in *Whither Mankind?* p. 139.
[3] Johnston. *Citizenship in the Industrial World*, p. 29.

beautiful hand work which have come down to us that such articles were in common use, whereas it is probable that the mass of people, if they possessed such articles at all, had to be content with examples of inferior quality that have long since disappeared.

Another important reminder comes from an account of Thomas Chippendale and eighteenth-century cabinet-making.

> " It is often argued that the craftsman of past centuries took a greater interest in his work than the modern man who lives in an age of machinery. In the former case it is assumed that the head, the heart and the hand worked together in unison. This theory contains something of truth and something of romance. . . . It would be natural to expect that a small cabinet maker whose work was the offspring of his own imagination and his own hand, should with an artist's pride watch his conception shaping itself into reality. But in a workshop, with 20 or 30 men at the bench, much division of labour would be found, and the efforts of an individual craftsman would no doubt be confined to the repetition of some detail which might have to be repeated time after time."[1]

Take again watch-making in French Switzerland before and after the introduction of peculiarly delicate machinery. There was already, before machinery came in, a considerable division of labour, and Marshall emphasises the fact that machinery displaced the work of operatives " who had indeed acquired a very high and specialised manual skill, but who lived sedentary lives, straining their eyesight through microscopes, and finding in their work very little scope for any faculty except a mere command over the use of their fingers." Then came

> " a beautiful machine which feeds itself with steel wire at one end, and delivers at the other tiny screws

[1] Oliver Brackett. *Chippendale and His Times*, cited by Gloag, *Artifex*, p. 84.

D

of exquisite form . . . and the person who minds it must have an intelligence and an energetic sense of responsibility, which go a long way towards making a fine character ; and which, though more common than they were, are yet sufficiently rare to be able to earn a high rate of pay. No doubt this is an extreme case ; and the greater part of the work of a watch-factory is much simpler. But a great deal of it requires higher faculties than the old system did, and those engaged in it earn, on the average, higher wages ; at the same time it has already brought the price of a trustworthy watch within the range of the poorest classes of the community and is showing signs of being able to accomplish the highest class of work."[1]

Here is a case where the earlier skill was that of manual dexterity, and where it gave place to a new kind of technical expertness and judgment. This example may also serve to illustrate another consideration that applies to many kinds of work in which accuracy is of the first importance. The earlier craftsman worked to a rough degree of accuracy guided by long practice and by trial and error. Mr. George Bourne describes the way in which the craft knowledge of the waggon-builder was acquired.

" It was set out in no book. It was not scientific. I never met a man who professed more than an empirical acquaintance with the waggon-builder's lore. My own case was typical. I knew that the hind-wheels had to be five feet two inches high and the fore-wheels four feet two ; that the ' sides ' must be cut from the best four-inch heart of oak, and so on. This sort of thing I knew, and in vast detail in course of time ; but I seldom knew why. And that is how most other men knew. The lore was a tangled network of country prejudices, whose reasons were known in some respects

---

[1] Marshall. *Economics of Industry*, Bk. IV, ch. ix, § 2.

here, in others there, and so on. In farmyard, in tap-room, at market, the details were discussed over and over again, they were gathered together for remembrance in village workshop ; carters, farmers, wheelmakers, in thousands handed on each his own little bit of understanding, passing it to his son or to the wheelwright of the day, linking up the centuries. But for the most part, the details were but dimly understood ; the whole body of knowledge was a mystery, a piece of folk-knowledge, residing in the folk collectively, but never wholly in any individual."[1]

" Our two-foot rules took us no nearer to exactness than the sixteenth of an inch : we used to make or adjust special gauges for the nicer work, but very soon a stage was reached when eye and hand were left to their own cleverness, with no guide to help them. So the work was more of an art—a very fascinating art— than a science, and in this art, as I say, the brain had its share. A good wheelwright knew by art and not by reasoning the proportion to keep between the spokes and felloes ; and so too, a good smith knew how tight a two-and-a-half-inch tyre should be for a four-foot wheel, and so on. He felt it, in his bones. It was a perception with him. But there was no science in it ; no reasoning. Every detail stood by itself and had to be learnt either by trial and error or by tradition."[2]

Attractive as this picture doubtless is, it must not blind us to the disadvantages both to the exactness of the work and to the mind of the worker, of the trial and error method, which often meant fumblings and failures, and still more often, teasing and trying annoyances. In point of accuracy, modern machinery has worked miracles. Mr. William Taylor, in his presidential address to the Institution of Mechanical Engineers in 1932, on " Mechanical Engineering applied to the making of

---

[1] *The Wheelwright's Shop*, pp. 73–74.   [2] *Ibid.*, pp. 19–20.

Lenses," spoke of the amazing degree of precision attained in the optical industry.

" For ordinary machining of metals the limit is about one thousandth of an inch, the fine tool or watch-maker must deal with one-ten-thousandth of an inch, but in the optical industry dimensions must be correct to between one hundred-thousandth and a few millionths of an inch. As Mr. Taylor suggested, the skill of the old maker of lenses was a thing of wonder, not on account of his conscious knowledge or of any deep thought which he put into his every action but because . . . he had . . . mainly from experience of many failures and some successes learned how to do good work as a matter of habit. Even his thinking had become routine thinking. The introduction of precision machinery has done nothing to eliminate a noble art, but has, instead, transmuted practice, based on inexact knowledge and tradition, into a scientific application of well-defined principles. What the machines have eradicated is drudgery—both mental and physical—and they leave the operator free to concentrate on the quality of his work."[1]

But while the application of scientific method has enabled us to achieve a far higher degree of accuracy, and has substituted exact knowledge and practice for hearsay and rule of thumb, it is not always and in every kind of operation capable as yet of replacing or improving on the methods empirically reached by the outstandingly skilled handicraftsman. Dr. Myers says that " it took a year or more of the highest technical research to formulate scientifically the valuable methods which had been traditionally used by a certain aged operative in a certain manufacturing process."[2]

Nor is the handicraftsman necessarily supplanted by

[1] *Manchester Guardian Commercial Supplement*, Nov. 5th, 1932. cf. Ford. *Moving Forward*, ch. XIV : "A Millionth of an Inch."

[2] *Business Rationalisation*, p. 10.

machinery. His work may be supplemented by machinery in ways that relieve him of toilsome and monotonous labour and make possible an easier and finer performance.   In Europe indeed, it is said that not only does the number of persons engaged in handicrafts still outweigh the number engaged in large-scale industry, but that the machine has actually created additional tasks for the hand skills.

" Large scale industry has provided certain old trades with the means of keeping alive and even of expanding.   It has created and nurtured a number of new handicrafts which flourish side by side with it, and which it has neither the will nor the power to absorb."[1]

In these cases, the machine often does the preliminary operations, and the hand-worker, as finisher, dresser or fitter, completes the job.

It must further be remembered that mass-production is not applicable to a great many industrial undertakings, and that factory work, whether mass-production or not, only accounts for a proportion probably less than 25 per cent. of the total area of employment.   Mr. Chase calculates that for the United States—the most highly mechanised country—in the year 1920 factory workers comprised less than eight millions out of $41\frac{1}{2}$ millions ' gainfully employed,' and that the total number of machine workers in or outside factories was about 10 millions, that is to say, about a quarter of the working population and 10 per cent. of the entire population of the United States.   He also calculates that not more than half of these could be considered ' unskilled ' machine workers, and that the number of ' net possible robots ' could not be more than 5 millions, that is, 5 per cent. of the total population and about 13 per cent. of those gainfully employed.[2] Moreover, since 1920 the pro-

---

[1] M. Rabinowitz in an article in the *International Labour Review*, cited by Chase, *Men and Machines*, p. 176.

[2] Chase. *Men and Machines*, pp. 145–147.

portion of factory workers has declined owing to the growth of automatic machinery, and the decline has been mainly in the number of ' unskilled ' or ' semi-skilled ' employed.   This tendency is borne out by other observations.   In the earlier stages of mass-production, the effect is " to evaporate skill from the lower reaches of industry and distil it in the upper reaches."[1]   But as time goes on more and more processes are handed over to automatic machinery, and the proportion of unskilled labour is reduced: It is interesting to compare Mr. Ford's earlier book, *My Life and Work* with his latest book, *Moving Forward*.   In the former he emphasises the small amount of skill and the small amount of training that the greater part of the work in his factories demanded, while in the latter he emphasises the increasing demand for skilled and highly trained workers.

"As we have learned more about economical manufacturing we have steadily cut out the jobs requiring brute force, and also we have cut out the jobs that required little or no intelligence, though we have never had a job of any kind for the unskilled man that did not require more acute perceptions than the rough jobs to which he had been accustomed as an unskilled labourer."[2]

" Modern industry demands more highly skilled men and more of them than are in the world to-day.   We are distinctly short of skilled men and one of the weaknesses of industry is that, in general, it has not been able to provide the facilities for training the army of men that are needed."[3]

" The situation is exactly the reverse of what it is commonly supposed to be, for, instead of industry requiring a constantly lessening proportion of skilled men, it is requiring a constantly growing proportion. These men require not only skill but versatility, and it is harder to get versatility than it is to get skill."[4]

[1] Pound. *Iron Man*, p. 22.   [2] *Moving Forward*, p. 121.
[3] *Ibid*, p. 134.   [4] *Ibid*, p. 135.

Mr. C. G. Renold of Manchester reports the same tendency in his own engineering works, where the proportion of highly skilled employment is constantly going up.

" The reducing of manufacture to mass production involves the development of an organisation of control, with a refinement of clerical methods, that introduces large new fields of skill. . . . What is happening is that skill which used to be applied to the production of articles of *direct* consumption is being eliminated and replaced by skill applied to the design and construction of the machinery and tools for making those articles ; to a more refined control of the raw material out of which they are made ; to the finding of markets for them ; and to the control of complex organisations."[1]

A study of the developments that have been taking place in industry shews both changes in the form of skill and the emergence of new skills.   Mr. J. W. F. Rowe, in his book on *Wages in Practice and Theory*, finds, for example, in the engineering industry, an increase of skill and accuracy among pattern-makers, a new class of ' semi-skilled ' workers in the foundry, where pneumatic hammers and riddles and electric cranes have eliminated the heavy work, and where the brass moulder, the loam and sand moulder and the core maker are, on the whole, more skilled than hitherto, and in spite of the disappearance of the ' all-round ' turner in the machine shop, a more specialised turner who has to work to more complicated designs with elaborate blue-prints.

The question of the place of skill in modern industry has been confused by a failure to distinguish different kinds and degrees of skill, and also by a tendency to confine attention to some one corner of industry or even to some particular period in that corner.   Different industries and different undertakings within those industries will be found to be at very different stages of

---

[1] *Economic Journal*, December, 1928.

development according to the place or the period that we observe. But the broad tendency would seem to be one that need cause no fear for the decline of skilled work, and though we may find many jobs that involve repetitive process work which is relatively unskilled, we may be sure that " the machine-feeders will in time be replaced by growing numbers of machine-minders, where higher qualities of skill and foresight are demanded,"[1] and that the proportion of skilled to unskilled workers will steadily increase.

Supplementary Note.

There are signs of a more thorough enquiry as to the best way in which the machine can supplement some of the older hand skills, especially among workers who have not yet become industrialised. Dr. Aldred Barker, Professor of Textile Industries in the University of Leeds, has made an investigation into the textile handicrafts of Kashmir. As a result, he has advised a policy midway between that of a complete suppression of the machine (which Mr. Gandhi advocates), and the imposition of a fully developed mechanised industry.

" Instead of fixing up a factory with looms and introducing a flock of workers to push on the starting handles, we might provide each worker with his own loom by a system of gradual purchase, make him feel that the machine belongs to him, and, above all, see that he understands it—that he knows he is controlling force and not working blindly. Here is probably a means of salvation for much modern industry."[2]

Dr. Barker, in the course of his enquiries, made a tour of the seats of our English hand industries, and of the old textile districts of Scotland and of the Shetland Islands, and makes an illuminating comment on his observations.

" Much as it may grieve some idealist friends, there

[1] Myers, *Business Rationalisation*, p. 30.
[2] *The Times*, Dec. 23rd, 1932.

is but one story to tell—of hardships under the old handicraft conditions and of improvement in social and economic life following the introduction of the industrialised system. Even the special industries of the Shetland Islands have to-day an industrial or mechanised basis, and beyond question the old handicrafts, as an economic proposition, have passed away."

In his report to the Maharajah's Government he has shown :

> " 1. That the spinning wheel will produce from four to eight times as much as the *Katwa* or distaff spindle.
>
> 2. That the machine will produce from 400 to 600 times as much per worker as the spinning wheel."

And his conclusions are of importance to those who desire hand-woven products.

> " Broadly speaking, the only claim to superiority of a hand-spun and hand-woven fabric is irregularity— if this can be considered a serious claim. But, if desirable, machine spinning and weaving can produce the irregularities of hand-spinning and hand-weaving, and in addition can spin and weave better than is possible by hand methods. That some machine products wear badly is not due to their being machine produced, but to the fact that the machine—working so perfectly—does give the opportunity for inferior fibres to be incorporated into very presentable yarns and fabrics. These remarks, of course, do not apply to the Kashmir shawls and carpets, which are a response to the desires of the connoisseur. Nor do they involve the suppression of any handicraft which may be practised for its own satisfaction.

> " Machine work, rightly dealt with, need not be soul-destroying at all, but may yield the three satisfactions we all desire—namely, the satisfaction of knowledge and insight, the satisfaction of skilful control, and the satisfaction of creation or production."

CHAPTER VI

INDUSTRIAL FATIGUE

IT is an ironical commentary on our industrial civilisation that the first systematic enquiry in Great Britain into the fatigue of the worker was undertaken not with a view to lightening the workers' toil but with a view to increasing the output of munitions for mechanical warfare. Towards the end of 1915 a Health of Munitions Workers' Committee was appointed " to consider and advise on questions of industrial fatigue, hours of labour and other matters affecting the personal health and physical efficiency of workers in munitions factories and workshops." Interim reports were issued containing recommendations for immediate changes and improvements, and the final report appeared in 1918. The opening pages of the final report unconsciously recall the advice that was given by Robert Owen a hundred years earlier.

" I have expended much time and capital upon improvements of the living machinery ; and it will soon appear that the time and money so expended in the manufactory at New Lanark . . . are now producing a return exceeding fifty per cent., and will shortly create profits equal to cent. per cent. on the original capital expended in them. Indeed, after experience of the beneficial effects from due care and attention to the mechanical implements, it became easy to a reflecting mind to conclude at once that at least equal advantage would arise from the same application of similar care and attention to the living instruments. And when it was perceived that inanimate mechanism was greatly improved by being made firm and substantial, that it was the essence of economy to keep it

neat, clean, regularly supplied with the best substance
to prevent unnecessary friction, and by proper supervision for the purpose to preserve it in good repair;
it was natural to conclude that the more delicate,
complex, living mechanism would be equally improved
by being trained to strength and activity; and that it
would also prove good economy to keep it neat and
clean; to treat it with kindness, that its mental movements might not experience too much irritating
friction; to endeavour by every means to make it more
perfect; to supply it regularly with a sufficient
quantity of wholesome food and other necessaries of
life, that the body might be preserved in good working
condition, and prevented from being out of repair, or
falling prematurely to decay."[1]

Compare that pronouncement of Robert Owen's in
1814 with this passage from the Report on the Health of
Munition Workers in 1918.

" The human being is a finely-adjusted physiological
instrument, which must no longer be wasted, much less
destroyed, by ignorant or wilful misuse. A working
man's capital is, as a rule, his health and his capacity
to perform a full day's work. Once that is impaired or
damaged beyond recuperation, two things happen.
First, his whole industrial outlook is jeopardised and
he becomes by rapid stages a liability and even a
charge upon the State. Secondly, if the bodily defence
is weakened by stress and strain, the man falls a victim
to disease, such as tuberculosis. . . . To secure
harmony and smooth working, to secure efficiency and
maximum output, the machine must be subservient to
the man; it is his individual health, mental development and moral well-being that is the guarantee of
effective labour."[2]

[1] *New View of Society*, Everyman's Edition, p. 9.
[2] *Final Report of Health of Munition Workers' Committee* (Cd.
9065), p. 7.

Since this Report was issued, the whole question has been under the observation of an Industrial Fatigue Research Board (now the Industrial Health Research Board) responsible to the Medical Research Council, and the Board's reports together with the reports of the National Institute of Industrial Psychology, contain a mass of evidence upon the subject. In spite of the volume of research, however, it is still impossible to say exactly what is fatigue. Fatigue, like toothache, is palpable but imponderable. We can only define it in terms of its effects, and it is usual to accept the definition proposed by Dr. Rivers : " a condition of lowered capacity for work which follows or occurs during the performance of work of which it is the direct result." It will be seen that his statement intentionally confines itself to what can be measured and tested, namely, ' capacity for work,' and avoids reference to physiological sensations or subjective feelings of being tired or exhausted. For the fact is that neither the sensations nor the ' feeling ' of fatigue are an adequate measure of the actual condition. It has been found, for example, that the effects of fatigue on the quantity and quality of work often occur before there is any definite sensation of fatigue. It is also a familiar experience that mental fatigue or boredom—accompanied by sensations of muscular tiredness—may be felt before there has been any strain on the muscles. The Health of Munitions Workers Committee declared that bodily sensations are a " fallacious guide to the true state of fatigue that may be present," and they therefore had recourse—for the purpose of ascertaining the presence and degree of fatigue—to objective tests relating to output of work, quality of work, liability to errors or spoilt work, liability to sickness and to accidents.

The effects of fatigue are measurable ; the remoter causes are often ascertainable, but the immediate causes or conditions are still obscure. It is, however, generally held that fatigue is not a question of " the simple using up or ' exhaustion ' of the substances supplying the chemical energy which is liberated during work, but of the accumulation within the living elements of the products of the chemical changes involved. Fatigue of the animal machine, that is to say, is not to be compared with the running down of a clock weight, but rather with the clogging of the wheel in some mechanism by dirt."[1] The chemical products which thus accumulate in the nervous system are removed by the blood " in part directly by irrigation, and in part, indirectly, through chemical changes in the tissue itself produced by constituents of the blood."[2]

Consequently, rest after work is not a purely passive condition, but an active process of chemical change and restoration of powers. Physiologists are still uncertain about the actual process of fatigue ' poisoning ' in the muscles. What appears to be more certain is that the primary expression of fatigue occurs not in the muscles themselves but higher up in the nervous system, possibly owing to some reflex inhibition of the central motor apparatus. In that case, fatigue is primarily a nervous factor, and may probably be considered as serving the function of a protective warning, designed to prevent bodily exhaustion. " It has been shewn definitely that when complete fatigue has been induced in a muscle, *so far as response to voluntary effort is concerned*, if the muscle or group of muscles thus fatigued be stimulated, a contraction of muscle will take place which may be as great as was the case at the outset of the experiment."[3] In other words, " fatigue in the nervous system outstrips in its onset fatigue in the muscles."[4] For this reason, work involving close attention, nice discrimination, and fine co-ordination of the senses, as of touch and sight, will begin to fall off in quantity and quality before there is

[1] *Report.* Section 53.   [2] *Report.* Section 54.
[3] Cathcart. *The Human Factor in Industry*, p. 19 (his italics).
[4] *Report.* Section 60.

actual sensation of muscular fatigue, and certainly before the muscles themselves are exhausted.

A further confirmation of the view that sensation is an inadequate measure of actual capacity for work comes from the study of the action of alcohol and other drugs, the subjective effects of which have little or no relation to the actual objective results. The researches of Rivers and others have shewn that under the influence of alcohol a man may feel an increase of energy and ease, and under the stimulus of increased confidence may for a time put forth more successful effort, but that the effect of the narcotic action of the alcohol is to impair the efficiency of his work. The drug dulls the sensations of fatigue, and is consequently welcomed by those who are feeling fatigued, but it tends also to weaken the capacity for finer discrimination and co-ordination of movements and thus to make errors and accidents more likely.

Increased liability to accidents is one of the signs of industrial fatigue. Many other factors may account for accidents. Apart from the dangers attaching to certain forms of work such as mining and dock labour, there are mechanical factors like inadequately fenced machinery, and personal factors like carelessness and inattention. It has been found that some people are ' accident-prone ' and researches are being conducted to enable such to be excluded from certain occupations by suitable selection tests.[1]

But fatigue, whether induced by overlong spells of work, by monotony, or by bad conditions of lighting or ventilation, is itself an important factor, and a high accident rate may often be taken as a sign of fatigue. It is significant that examination of diagrams representing the curve of frequency of accidents over various spells of work reveals in many cases that the number of accidents increases in the morning to a maximum between the hours of 10 and

---

[1] Welch and Miles. *Industrial Psychology in Practice*, pp. 139, 142-5.

12 and in the afternoon to a maximum between the hours of 4 and 6. The fact that the accident rate often falls again in the final working hour may be partly due to the revival of energy that accompanies the prospect of an early release from work and is known as ' end-spurt,' and partly to the accompanying decline of output (which, in spite of end-spurt, may occur from various causes during the period).

But the most reliable evidence of fatigue is to be found in actual output of work. Diagrams of work curves reveal certain familiar features. At the beginning of the spell there is a ' warming-up ' period in which one is ' getting into practice,' and which may be accompanied by or followed by an ' initial spurt ' or ' incitement ' rise. This will be followed by a more level run (or ' plateau ') during which the output will be maintained at the maximum of efficiency (sometimes known as ' settlement '). Then a decline sets in, presumably due to fatigue—physical or mental—and the curve will drop to the end of the spell, unless revived by ' end-spurt.' There will be variations in this curve according to the kind of work that is in question—the extent to which it is strenuous muscular work, or work involving dexterity and close attention, or again work that is highly mechanised and automatic.[1]

Similar changes may be noted in the volume and efficiency of work according to the day or part of the week. After a holiday the period of ' warming up ' is more prolonged, and the ' Monday effect ' or ' Blue Monday ' is a well-known phenomenon. The middle of the week will usually show the best results and then a decline will be experienced toward the end of the week, varied by a possible ' end-spurt ' on the Friday—approaching pay-time. It would appear likely that overtime is best arranged, where possible, toward the beginning rather than the end of the week. It is also probable that the

---

[1] Myers. *Mind and Work*, p. 62.

Saturday morning might well be dropped in many undertakings since for many reasons the results are not commensurate with the cost. The five-day week of 45 hours has been tried successfully in a number of firms in both America and Czechoslovakia, and output has been maintained or increased in most cases.[1]

All that has been said indicates the importance of considerable periods of rest and recreation. For a time during the war men munition workers were employed on Sundays, but the Health of Munition Workers Enquiry condemned the practice. They shewed that the evidence as to both the quantity and quality of work where Sunday labour was in force supported the famous argument of Macaulay in his speech on the Ten Hours Bill in 1846.

" That day is not lost. While industry is suspended, while the plough lies in the furrow, while the Exchange is silent, while no smoke ascends from the factory, a process is going on quite as important to the wealth of nations as any process which is performed on more busy days. Man, the machine of machines, the machine with which all the contrivances of the Watts and the Arkwrights are worthless, is repairing and winding up, so that he returns to his labours on the Monday with clearer intellect, with livelier spirits, with renewed corporal vigour. Never will I believe that what makes a population stronger and healthier, wiser and better, can ultimately make it poorer."[2]

The same argument may be used to support the case for a shorter working week. The pioneer experiment in the 48-hour week was carried out by Mather and Platt at the Salford Iron Works in 1893. They were able to report both shortly afterwards and at the end of a decade that production had been improved. The later progress in the adoption of the 48 hours week has shewn not only

[1] *I.L.O. Report on Social Aspects of Rationalisation*, Series B, No. 18, p. 153.
[2] *Report of Health of Munition Workers' Committee*, Section 44.

improvements in output, but also reduction in the amount of ' lost time ' through various causes, including sickness.[1] Not only a shorter working week, but also longer holidays with pay, would probably represent an economy in what Professor Sargent Florence calls " the business costs of industrial inefficiency "—costs in absence, ill-health, accidents, deficient output and unrest.[2] But, apart from week-end and other holidays, the introduction of rest-pauses during spells of work has been found to be advantageous. Investigations carried out by the Industrial Fatigue Research Board " consistently suggest that the judicious introduction of rest-pauses of 10 to 15 minutes into a spell of $4\frac{1}{2}$ to 5 hours will eventually be followed by an increase in output of the order of 5 to 10 per cent. nothwithstanding the shorter time actually worked."[3] The best time to introduce such pauses is just before the fall in the work curve is due to occur, so as to ward off the fatigue as far as possible. The length of the pause will be determined by experiment in relation to the kind of work involved : it is clear that the pause must be long enough to afford relief, but not so long as to make it difficult to resume work. It is considered that organised pauses taken by all the workers at the same time are more effective than either enforced delays due to failure of machinery or supplies, or voluntary pauses taken by the individual workman often furtively and without sanction and, consequently, without full relaxation.

But, while the advantages of an organised and uniform rest-pause are obvious, it is also obvious that the individual worker is not actually fatigued or bored at the same time as his fellows, and that the organised rest-pause can only be arranged to meet a rough and ready measure of average requirements. How far can the organised rest - pause

[1] Myers, *Industrial Psychology in Great Britain*, p. 60.
[2] See his *Economics of Fatigue and Unrest*, ch. 5.
[3] *Fifth Annual Report of Industrial Fatigue Research Board*, 1925, p. 25.

E

meet the condition that is described in the following words of a worker in an electrical equipment machine shop ?

" There is often an intense desire to leave one's machine and have a walk round, which is compelled by three things—in the first place, by physical fatigue, which calls for periodic ' stretching ' of the legs, secondly, as a momentary escape from the noise, and thirdly, as an escape from the monotony of one's task and the unlovely surroundings—just to feel the wind and see the sky and see the passing faces of fellow-beings.

" But escape is seldom possible. One is even clocked into and out of the lavatory. The worker will search for any excuse to go away for a brief spell— ' more waste wanted,' ' a drink of water,' ' a spanner ' ; but sharp words or looks, and even dismissal await him if he is caught snatching a smoke, or across at another machine talking to one of his workmates."

It will be noted that the writer refers not only to the work itself as something from which he longs to escape for a moment, but also to the ugly and noisy conditions of the work. It is true that he is probably more sensitive to beauty and therefore to ugliness and clamour than many of his workmates. But people are unconsciously affected by conditions which they may never wittingly have noticed, and " our nature is subdu'd " not only " to what it works in " but to the atmosphere and surroundings among which it works. Plato speaks of " those who are reared among images of evil as in a foul pasture," and who " day by day and little by little, gather many impressions from all that surrounds them, taking them all in until at last a great mass of evil gathers in their inmost souls, and they know it not."[1] And apart from such incalculable and immeasurable effects, there is evidence

---

[1] *Republic*, 401.

that conditions like lighting, ventilation and noise, play a considerable part in the causation of fatigue.

Lighting. Not only inadequate lighting, but lighting accompanied by strong glare and deep shadow, is found to affect both quantity and quality of work, and "the position of the source of light is a factor quite as important as its intensity."[1] Care in the distribution of light, in the avoidance of glare, both direct and reflected, and in the cleanliness and brightness, not only of windows but of walls, ceilings, machines and fittings, mean a reduction in errors, accidents and waste. "Dirty windows represent a direct tax on production."[2] It is obviously easier to provide good lighting conditions in a factory or mill than in a mine or steel-works, and it is among miners and steel workers that I have found most frequent complaints on the score of eye-strain.

Ventilation. Here, the modern factory has greatly improved, and methods of ventilation, such as circulating-fans, are being adopted, which provide for the circulation of air (since even the purest air, if it be stagnant, is relaxing). An electrical worker tells me that concrete floors are hot to the feet in summer and freezing cold in winter, and suggests that it would be a boon to many workers who stand at a bench or machine to have wooden foot-boards. Dust and fumes are not only fatiguing but detrimental to health, and suction ventilators and vacuum exhausts are required for their elimination.[3] The weaving shed presents a special problem, because of the humidity and high temperature required (between 60 deg. and 80 deg. Fahrenheit). Still more difficult to regulate are the semi-outdoor jobs—in mine, for example, or steel works, or the cab of a railway engine. A miner undergoes extreme variations of temperature : "There was no central heating," says one of my informants, "the heat I experienced was the heat of the earth's

---

[1] Welch and Miles. *op. cit.*, p. 96.   [3] *Ibid,* p. 97.
[2] Welch and Miles. *op. cit.*, p. 121

bowels, and the heat from the sweating bodies of men and horses." In parts of the mine where the ventilation is poor, the atmosphere may be "terribly hot," says another, and also gas-laden. "In such a place, if you sat down for a rest or to have a meal, the heavy atmosphere would overpower you and make you feel very drowsy." The provision of pithead baths for miners under the Miners' Welfare Fund has been beneficial to health and has reduced the amount of time lost owing to sickness.

"Before the baths were installed, the men often reached the mine on a wet morning with soaked clothes, in which they had to work all day. Now, they change into warm, dry working clothing, and their clean clothes are dried for donning at the end of the shift. Similarly, when men are working in wet ' places,' they do not require to tramp or cycle the two miles home in wet clothing—in cold weather, an experience to test the hardiest of frames. It was a common experience for a miner to arrive home from work with his clothing stiffly frozen."[1]

A steel works will provide extremes of heat and cold. A man who has been employed as door-man on furnaces, as gripper and ingot trimmer, and as bar-loader, writes as follows :

"I found it very trying in the summer, sometimes it got beyond endurance and I had to stop working to recover. Perspiration literally poured from us all and our clothing became limp, sopping rags, even our boots squelched as we walked. During the colder weather it was better, but if we had stoppages due to breakages, etc., we were forced to huddle round the furnaces to keep warm."

A railway-engine fireman has told me of the changes in temperature that he has experienced on night work in the

[1] Mr. J. H. Mitchell, in *The Worker's Point of View* (*A Symposium*), p. 102.

summer when he has walked home in the cool night air in a dripping shirt. The cab of an engine, he says,

"is naturally a warm place to work in, but it can also be cold in the winter, especially to the feet. The draught from between the engine and tender is responsible for this. If one can put one's head out of the cab, or open the cab window a little, plenty of fresh air can be obtained. But in wet weather, when this is impossible, one is forced to breathe hot air which makes one dry and stuffy."

Noise. While lighting and ventilation are actually better under most machine conditions than in the days of the domestic workshop, and owe a great deal to mechanised inventions and especially to electricity, noise is a factor that has seriously increased. Recent investigations have shewn, however, the remarkable extent to which men become 'adapted' to noisy conditions of life and work. Two studies in the psychological effects of noise have been published by the Industrial Health Research Board, the one reporting experimental investigations in a laboratory, the other, observations in a workshop. In the former the attempt was made to isolate noise as a factor from other factors. The experiments shew that the initial effects of noise must be distinguished from its later effects.

"There is generally an initial disturbance which is usually counteracted by increase of effort, either voluntary or non-voluntary, but following this comes a definite period of adaptation. During that period the organism appears to settle down to the noisy conditions, treating them as a kind of natural background of its task, so that in many cases even the subjective discomfort diminishes or passes away. So much is this the case that any sudden qualitative change, e.g., from noise to silence, has a more disturbing effect upon performance than minor changes in the noise background itself."[1]

Non-synchronous noises were found to disturb the rhythm of motor performance, except when the latter had become automatised. The effects on the work of 'mental' as well as 'manual' workers were found to be surprisingly slight, and "13 of the 22 subjects who reported continuous or strong distraction, nevertheless did no worse, and in some instances a little better, with noise than without, and 5 of the 10 subjects who reported marked irritation did no worse under noisy than under silent conditions."[2] The reports were very conflicting, and "the only two points about which there was any considerable agreement were that rhythmic sounds might help automatic work, but mental work of any difficulty was best done in silence, and that loud irregular mechanical noise was always initially displeasing and disturbing."[3]

An experiment in the provision of 'ear-defenders' for the workers in a noisy weaving shed also shewed very varying results, but

> "there is some indication that those individuals who are most conscious of the distracting influence of noise show the greatest improvement in performance when the noise intensity is reduced. It is also apparent that among those who definitely believe themselves to be unaffected by noise, some at least show an appreciable improvement in output when ear-defenders are worn."[4]

The results as a whole suggested "that noise is detrimental to personal efficiency, even if it is assumed that its true effect on production in the present case is less than one per cent."; and it is also apparent that "even after years of work in a noisy environment, the worker does not become completely adapted or acclimatised to

[1] *Report,* p. 29.
[2] *Report,* p. 48.
[3] *Report,* p. 29.
[4] *Report,* p. 48.

noise but goes through the process of adaptation daily."[1]

It needs to be remembered that " even where noise has no measurable effect on health or output, it is possible that it may lead to an increased expenditure of nervous energy and thus ultimately to fatigue."[2] Moreover, there are always likely to be some individuals who suffer more than others from the effects of noise. A weaver of my acquaintance (who, I suspect, was originally unsuited for the work), tells me that he found the noise " unbearable." " Most weavers," (he says), " are entirely oblivious to the noise, but I had eventually to leave the work after an eight-months' nervous breakdown as a result of it." Further, there are types of work in which noise may be peculiarly nerve-racking and, indirectly, dangerous. Miners tell me that the rattling of coal-wagons and the noise of machinery in the pit is a strain upon the nerves because it becomes difficult for them to detect the first signs of a roof-breakage.

The effect of clatter may sometimes be detected in the liability of the worker in a noisy workplace to be irritated by disturbing noises outside the workplace (for example, in the home), although apparently unaffected by the noisier conditions of the work. This is difficult to test, but I cite the following observations of a smith's striker in a boiler yard :

" Boiler yards are notoriously noisy. . . . The clatter of hammers on steel plates, some being rivetted, some being levelled with heavy sledges on steel blocks, the staccato ear-piercing ' rat-tat ' of pneumatic hammers on hollow steel barrels, the whirring of belts and the drone of machinery combine to make an indescribable din. Prolonged conversation was something of a strain, and during the noisiest period, only possible when in close physical proximity to each other. Nevertheless, we did manage to talk a good deal.

[1] *Report*, p. 58.   [2] Welch and Miles, *op. cit.*, p. 134.

Some of the older men suffered from what is known as 'boilermakers' deafness,' and could, in fact, hear better in the shop than out. Both my father and I agreed that any outward noise at home was inclined to be irritating after a particularly noisy day in the shop."

It would appear in fact, that the process of adaptation to particular kinds of din may make a person more and not less sensitive to other forms of noise. An electrical wireman tells me the following story by way of illustration :—

"I was once working near a 100-ton hammer. Amid sulphurous air, and shriek of escaping steam, this huge block thumped down upon the red hot billets of steel with clank and thunderous noise—but the hammer-man turned to me and said, 'For God's sake, stop that whistling, it gets on my nerves !'"

Another point is illustrated by that story. We are liable to be more consciously irritated by irrelevant sounds than by those which are connected with the work we are doing. Mr. Chase observes that more annoying and fatiguing than typewriter or telephone in an office is the scraping of chair legs on the hard composition floor, and many of us would agree. Here the question of quality of sound also enters, and it is obvious that sounds of a certain *timbre*, or sounds that are discordant as well as unrhythmical, are inherently unpleasant to many people. Harsh bells and raucous voices will disturb far more than other noises, however loud and insistent.

A miner who has worked a haulage engine writes :—

"I was never particularly disturbed by the noise. As a matter of fact, the hum of the electrical motor and even the hiccoughy vent of the blast engine I found pleasant rather than disturbing sounds. Certain bells, I found, had a very disturbing and irritating effect upon me. I always hated working to a harsh discordant signal. Many times, in order to minimise the tone of the bell, I've held the gong tightly with my fingers and counted the number of beats registered against them and thus made out the signal."

It is also common experience that we are less disturbed by noises for which we are directly or indirectly responsible than by those contributed by other people—whether it be tearing calico, scratching a slate, starting up a motor cycle, or working a steam hammer or pneumatic drill.

A packer in an electrical factory says :—

"At first I found the noise in a factory intensely irritating, but after a time that wore off, and I found it more irritating if there was not a continual noise. Any unusual noise is distracting and nerve-racking, unless one happens to be making the noise oneself, when it doesn't seem to have any effect, except on other people."

A miner writes :—

"It was much better to be controlling, directing, or working on the machine causing the noise, than to be doing some other job away from it. If you were working the machine, the noise seemed to pass by you, it was a part of your work, it was a part of the machine you were working.

But if you were doing something near to the machine, but not directly connected with it, the noise caused a severe strain, it irritated and distracted you. It was noise under those circumstances which ruined my nerves for work down the mine. For three days I had to work near a powerful pump driven by compressed air, which exhausted irregularly with a shattering roar which echoed and re-echoed far worse than any clap of thunder in that confined space. At the end of each day my fellow-worker and I went home absolutely exhausted, with our nerves in shreds."

This points to the need of giving more consideration to the effect of noise, not only upon the worker immediately engaged on a noisy machine, but upon his fellow-workmen or others in the neighbourhood, and it is to be hoped that the Correspondence Committee on Industrial Hygiene of the International Labour Office, which has already recognised the injurious effect of noise on health, output and labour turnover,[1] will give further attention to this aspect.

[1] See *Brochure*, No. 129.

CHAPTER VII

MONOTONY AND BOREDOM

WE have been dealing with factors that make for nervous tension rather than fatigue in the ordinary meaning of the word. Most of those whom I have questioned lay stress on the irksomeness and wearisomeness of their work rather than its toilsomeness. There are, it is true, still jobs like those of the colliery putter, the coal-heaver, the railway-engine fireman, the stevedore, which are heavy and exhausting, but the larger proportion of jobs are tedious rather than toilsome.

This brings us to the special kind of fatigue that we may call ' mental ' as distinct from muscular or nervous fatigue, and which arises most often from monotony rather than over-work or pressure. It were, perhaps, more accurate to speak, not of ' mental fatigue ' but of the mental factor in fatigue, for we have already seen that mental, nervous and muscular fatigue are for the most part indistinguishable, both in symptoms and effects. Yet the subjective condition of ' boredom ' is as familiar and indubitable as it is elusive and imponderable. And it may accelerate or retard the other symptoms of fatigue. It is possible to go on working at an interesting task or playing an exciting game up to, if not beyond, a point that would otherwise be exhausting, without feeling mentally fatigued. It is equally possible to succumb to boredom—and in consequence, even to experience sensations of muscular tiredness, long before there can have been any strain on the muscular system. Dr. J. H. Hadfield has described an interesting experiment shewing the effect of ' suggestion ' on the energy of the human body. He tested three men with a dynamometer (1) in normal waking condition, (2) after applying the hypnotic suggestion of ' weakness,' and (3) after applying the hypnotic suggestion of ' great strength.'   The results were for (1) an average grip of 101 lbs., for (2) an average grip of only 29 lbs., and for (3) an average grip of 142 lbs.[1]

This experiment illustrates the importance of a mental factor like confidence in promoting human energy. Emotional excitement also serves to reinforce energy to the extent of making possible remarkable performances of strength and prowess.   People are capable of unexpected feats of strength and endurance when they are ' keyed up ' to an emergency.   William James, in his essay on *The Energies of Men*, argued that the most of us live for most of the time below our energy income.

> " In exceptional cases we find, beyond the very extremity of fatigue distress, amounts of ease and power that we never dreamed ourselves to own—sources of strength habitually not taxed at all, because habitually we never push through the obstruction, never pass the critical points."[2]

The experiments of Cannon and others suggest that the secretions of the adrenal glands play a considerable part in the experience of enhanced strength arising from emotional excitement.   These glands secrete more rapidly under emotions like fear and rage, strengthen the heart-action and quicken the circulation, and cause the liver to discharge stored glycogen[3] into the blood.   Thus the muscles obtain an increase of oxygen and also an increase of glycogen—their best fuel.   The process counteracts fatigue and reinforces energy.

Experiments, not only upon animals, but upon Uni-

---

[1] Dr. Hadfield's essay on *The Psychology of Power* in the Symposium, *The Spirit*.

[2] See the volume of Essays entitled *Memories and Studies*, p. 230.

[3] A carbohydrate closely allied to sugar and the starches.   See Crowden, *Muscular Work, Fatigue and Recovery*, p. 15.

versity students before and during examinations and before a football match, shewed an increase in the quantity of glycogen in the blood, and a preparatory increase even in the reserve players for the match.[1]

When we consider those conditions under which an extra effort is put forth, we realise the importance of emotional factors in furthering or hindering effective work.

A correspondent writes of his war-time experience :—

" Filling sand-bags and building new trenches far behind the lines was a dull and unexciting job and one which led rapidly to fatigue. In a trench, on the other hand, that was being heavily bombarded, one filled sand-bags for hours, throwing them into the gaps in the parapet made by shells without any feeling of fatigue at all."

Both quantity and quality of work will depend on either its intrinsic interest or the action of indirect energising motives. Lack of interest, on the other hand, as well as the lack of actuating or sustaining motives, will have a debilitating and depressing effect.

The most utterly boring of all conditions is that of purposeless inactivity. This is the bane of unemployment, and produces the *ennui* that afflicts the workless, whether rich or poor. Money may provide a measure of relief from this condition by the purchase of amusement or of travel, and the lot of the unemployed worker is made worse not only by anxiety and want, but by restriction of entertainment and of movement. This explains, also, the peculiar boredom of the under-employed, or even of those who are kept waiting for work by temporary breakdowns of machinery. A film studio hand who finds the work absorbingly interesting, tells me that the periods of waiting about are extremely trying.

" I found the work most exhausting when there was nothing to do. Sometimes, owing to a technical hitch,

---

[1] Cannon. *Bodily Changes in Pain, Hunger, Fear and Rage.*

the whole studio staff would be hanging about for hours doing nothing and when it was time to start again, I invariably felt too tired to carry on for long."

How far are the conditions of machine work of such a kind as to produce feelings of boredom and lack of interest and, consequently, to fail to elicit the best of which a man is capable ? This is a question on which no general answer can be given, because machine work is of so many kinds. In some forms of machine work the interest is so absorbing that monotony is at a minimum. A turner who works at an automatic lathe in a shop which produces the jigs, dies, and sundry kinds of small tools which are used in mass-production, writes to tell me : " I am rarely fatigued and never bored." On the other hand, a screen-hand, employed in separating dirt from coal on a continuous conveyor in a coal mine writes : " I am just as bored at the beginning of a shift as I am at the end of it." Between these two extremes are innumerable degrees of interest and boredom according to the nature of the work and the nature of the worker. For work that to one kind of temperament is distasteful, is to another endurable, if not pleasant. Even the repetition work of a highly sub-divided mass-production process will be found to affect the workers engaged in it in very different ways. A job that appears to the onlooker excessively mechanical and tedious is not always so to the worker, and conversely, a job that appears interesting at first sight, may well have become boring to the worker who has been engaged upon it for a long period. Moreover, it must be remembered that there is non-mechanical repetition work that may be exceedingly monotonous. A Post Office sorter of 45 writes :—

" I am not the only one who finds sorting letters for three or four hours a paralysing process. Some four or five young men have told me at different times they felt like ' jumping up and screaming ' or as though impelled to rush all round the place like madmen for a change. I find, for my part, that when I reach this stage of fatigue, I become malevolent. . . . Overseers, who may be casual observers, become warders, and as my exasperation pervades my whole mind, they become ominously intimidating, affrighting, full of malicious, overbearing devilry. I have no idea how, and to what extent, this state of mind affects my work ; I do know it is not likely to make me a good worker or a good citizen."

It is probable that the more intelligent the worker the more he will find a repetition task distasteful, though even here there are exceptions, for some workers would prefer a virtually automatic task that left them free to think about more interesting things to a job requiring close attention. But there are few jobs that permit the mind to wander entirely with immunity from hitch or accident, and most of those who appear to be satisfied with repetitive tasks are among the less intelligent and less imaginative. Mr. Ford probably exaggerates the number of workers who prefer mechanical work without initiative or responsibility or even any degree of skill.

" Repetitive labour—the doing of one thing over and over again and always in the same way—is a terrifying prospect to a certain kind of mind. It is terrifying to me. I could not possibly do the same thing day in and day out, but to other minds, perhaps I might say, to the majority of minds, repetitive operations hold no terrors."[1]

Mr. Ford does not seem to realise that the assertion that men adapt themselves contentedly to merely routine work is itself a confession of failure.

If work were to become purely mechanical and automatic, it is a question whether it were better to assign it to mentally defective workers, or to those who were

---

[1] *My Life and Work,* p. 103.

capable of pursuing an independent train of thought. But in the stage of mechanisation that is rapidly approaching there are likely to be fewer jobs of a purely routine character, and it is no longer possible to say either that mechanisation puts a premium on mental deficiency,[1] or on the other hand, that it frees the mind for intellectual or imaginative activity.

For most work to-day involves at least the intermittent application of close attention, and that, not at the time and discretion of the worker, but at the behest of the machine itself. The old time cobbler or tailor, working in his domestic workshop in a leisurely fashion, had some opportunity for thinking out his political or theological problems, and many a radical politician or nonconformist lay-preacher prepared his speeches or his sermons at the bench.

But the speeding up and regimentation of modern factory production, as well as the irregular and unpredictable occasions of the calls upon the workers' attention, allow to few workers the opportunity for sustained thinking or for more than fitful day-dreams. The more routine forms of mass-production process-work may permit the mind to range, but it is an exceptional type of mass-production worker who writes to me :—

" I have painted pictures, built cabinets, drafted essays and speeches, organised meetings, and a hundred other things in my mind whilst at the bench, and then there only remained the dull process of interpreting my finished plans into a more concrete medium. Time passed much quicker, and the work was always less wearisome, when I was solving some knotty problem of construction in connection with my several interests."

Workers engaged in other kinds of routine operation, clerical work or accountancy, for example, occasionally

---

[1] Compare, e.g., Mr. Pound's phrase : " The Iron Man is a consistent friend of the defective."

indulge in day-dreams, and one of them tells me that when he caught himself day-dreaming he would go back to the last page of figures he remembered to have checked and go over the additions again, "but I have *never* detected myself in a mistake in day-dreaming," and then he tells me that the principal of a firm of accountants gave the same testimony.

But the machine worker who day-dreams is in danger of more than a mistake in calculation, and several of my informants emphasise the perils of distraction.

"Sometimes," says one, "I have been lulled into a sense of security only to be brought back to earth by the sudden cognisance of either a perfectly absurd action, or one that, but for good fortune, might have been fraught with dire consequences to myself. But one rarely mentions these incidents."

A printer was less fortunate.

"In 'flat work' I very often used to day-dream. The purely mechanical action of picking up a sheet of paper, and setting it against 'marks' all day long, brings about a state of coma. . . . Click, pick the sheet up. Bang, air it (make the air go under it by a flick of the wrist). Shush, bring the sheet to the 'marks.' Here the machine takes it. Repeat this all day long, eight hours a day, forty-eight hours a week, and you may be able to visualise the effect on the mind. It was on these machines that I day-dreamed, until I had the good luck to put my hand in instead of the paper. I say good luck, because it happened to be a small machine, and I was able to brake it quickly. In fact, by taking my hand, it stopped itself. I had to have the top of one finger grafted on, and several of the bones in the hand re-set. Needless to say, I never day-dream now."

Coalminers have told me of the dangers of day-dreaming in the mine. "If I day-dreamed," says one,

F

" I generally paid dearly for it.   Some chaps paid for it with their lives."   " Day-dreamers," says another, " very soon receive one of the following : (a) an accident (b) the sack."   Day-dreaming, whether dangerous or not, is the common resource of the repetition-worker.   The work is sufficiently mechanical to relieve the mind from constant attention, but too pressing or subject to slight interruptions for sustained thinking.   " It takes little physical energy," says one of my informants, " and demands just sufficient concentration to prevent one from thinking much of other things."   Discontinuous picture-thinking takes place under these conditions.   The worker finds himself picturing some incident in the past or speculating (sometimes in more than one sense) upon the future.

Various expedients are employed to relieve the monotony of repetitive work.   Conversation,[1] singing and whistling are not always discouraged, and in some workshops provision is made by the management for singing or for gramophone music.   A change of operation or of posture may also be facilitated.   The Industrial Fatigue Research Board report that " it appears uneconomical to maintain the same form of unbroken activity throughout the spell of work, yet too many changes in the form of activity are equally undesirable."[2]   Even changes of posture are a help—for example, from a sitting to a standing position, or *vice versa*—in alleviating not only monotony but physical fatigue.   This is a point to remember when considering the advice of ' efficiency ' experts to eliminate every kind of superfluous movement. The psychologist, here as elsewhere, has often to correct the assumptions of the ' efficiency ' expert.   Unnecessary movements or movements that might be eliminated by a more orderly assemblage of tools, materials, etc., may often serve a valuable purpose, just because they relieve

---

[1] Opportunities of course vary enormously.   In a noisy workshop it may be carried on by lip-reading.

[2] *Report*, No. 26.

the monotony of routine employment.   For that reason
they may sometimes be less wasteful in the long run than
some of the ostensibly ' anti-waste ' devices which keep
the worker immovably confined to a single position and
a single set of movements.

But boredom arises from other factors than the performance of repeated operations.   Monotony of employment rather than monotony of movement is responsible
for the greater part of boredom.   Employers who are
concerned to diminish their ' labour turnover ' have found
that the provision of opportunities for transfer from one
department to another often yields remarkable results
both by relieving monotony and by enabling workers to
discover the kind of work in which they can do their best
and find most interest.

But while mechanical routine work is monotonous, there
is a great deal of machine work that is neither exhausting
nor boring.   It is tiresome rather than tiring, and apt to
produce annoyance rather than *ennui*.   Dr. Pear has used
the word ' irksome ' to describe such work.   Many tasks,
he says,

> " are not boring, for they demand close unbroken
> attention and they cannot be performed mechanically.
> They are not fatiguing ; each one lasts only for a short
> time ; in fact their irksomeness may consist in the fact
> that so many changes have to be made that ' one can
> never settle down to anything '.   They are just con-
> sistently unpleasant."[1]

Such tasks are by no means confined to machine work.
As Dr. Pear says, " any housewife will give dozens of
examples."   Machinery indeed has relieved us of many
forms of irksome as well as toilsome labour, but machine
work itself is developing its own irksome operations, and
it may well be that many workers would prefer the more
wearisome forms of routine work to the more irksome

---

[1] *Fitness for Work*, pp. 126–127.

forms of work that demand " close unbroken attention."

The skilled worker who is engaged on intricate points of detail experiences a special kind of nervous fatigue. An electrical wireman writes :—

" The fatigue of nerves was apparent, particularly in the assembly rooms where one is engaged upon small detail work. Small screws and intricate corners produced a peculiar tingling in the hands, up to the arms, the shoulder blades, and across the forehead. It appears to be a nervous tension producing irritation, consequent upon (a) continual close contact and manipulation of the hands, and (b) the habit of one's eyes, or at least of *my* eyes, which after gazing at the twiddling fingers and detailed work before me, suddenly shift their focus to ' infinity ' and stare *past* my work, inducing a certain befuddlement in my brain, which is often dispelled by a shake of the head."

The increasing demand for skilled attention to the design, repair and maintenance of machinery may be expected to add to the number of irksome operations. But apart from the nervous strain of work demanding close attention and fine manipulation, there is always a large amount of irksome drudgery even in the most ' interesting' occupations, and the illustrations I have given may serve to remind us, first, that an outsider's impression of a job is apt to be misleading, and second, that there is no job which has not its wearisome and irksome periods. Mr. Harold Nicolson, reviewing Mr. Compton Mackenzie's third instalment of *Greek Memories*, writes :—

" The unobservant reader might study this book without recognising the Secret Service as the drab and dowdy thing it is. He might be left with the impression of motor boats foaming out into the Ægean, of powerful Bentleys roaring through the thyme-scented night of Attica, of strong men grasping revolvers, while the feet of their enemies sounded on the stairs. Such incidents occur but rarely. The true picture of any Director of Secret Intelligence would be the picture of a man, with a cup of luke-warm tea beside him, fiddling with endless files."[1]

It will never be possible to eliminate an element of drudgery in any occupation. Scientists, artists, and athletes as well as professional and industrial workers are bound to put in long hours of wearisome and irksome labour. Think of the patient experimental observation and statistical recording of the scientist, the regular and unremitting ' practice ' of the musician or the dancer, the indefatigable attention to recurring details of the mother, the nurse, and the school teacher. A long-range interest and purpose sustains them over the stretches and *longueurs* of bothersome and sometimes barren effort. How far industry can supply such interest and elicit such devotion is a question that must be held over for later consideration.

[1] *New Statesman and Nation*, Oct. 29th, 1932.

CHAPTER VIII

THE conditions of machine work and the contacts of the worker with machinery are extremely varied. The mental make-up of the worker is moreover infinitely various. Differences of intelligence, aptitude, temperament, up-bringing, education, locality and previous industrial experience—all go to produce an immense diversity of reactions to work and workshop conditions. We may expect, then, to find as many opinions of machinery as there are kinds of machine-work and kinds of machine-worker. If we attempt here to set down some typical reactions, it must be remembered that they are only representative of certain types, and that there are wide variations within as well as beyond each type.

Mr. Stuart Chase has drawn attention to the different kinds of contact with machinery that are possible to-day, and pointed out that " certain machine contacts are as lethal as others are wholesome and invigorating."[1] He has also reminded us that factory machines have passed through certain stages of development, though any given factory to-day may be in the early stages. We have already seen that the process of subdivision which replaced certain forms of skilled work by semi-skilled or unskilled repetitive work has in turn replaced certain forms of semi-skilled or unskilled work by automatic machinery. As this stage develops, the skilled man more and more " comes back into the picture, as inspector, repairer, adjuster of delicate controls."[2] Moreover, as

[1] *Men and Machines*, p. 116.
[2] *Ibid.*, p. 104.

this phase of mechanisation develops, machinery evokes more and more interest and less and less hostility among those directly concerned in its operation.[1] These developments, to which Mr. Stuart Chase and M. Henri De Man call attention, do not, however, take place as an inevitable and invariable sequence, and the writers have been, I suspect, over-much preoccupied with the engineering industry.

But whatever be the course of development of machine-production in any industry, it is clear that there is a profound difference between work which is dominated by the speed and requirements of machinery and work which involves some control over the speed. The worker engaged in the first type of machine work is impressed by his own impotence and relative unimportance. He feels himself dominated by the insistent and relentless demands of the machine, its unrelaxing and untiring drive. This was one of the earliest complaints against the factory system. The Hammonds quote an account of a Manchester cotton mill written in 1832 :—

" Whilst the engine runs the people must work—men, women and children are yoked together with iron and steam. The animal machine—breakable in the best case, subject to a thousand sources of suffering—is chained fast to the iron machine, which knows no suffering and no weariness."[2]

To the question how the ' young persons ' were kept steadily to their work a witness before the Children's Employment Commission of 1865, replied :—

" They cannot well neglect their work ; when they once begin, they must go on ; they are just the same as parts of a machine."[3]

It was that aspect of factory work that stirred the pity and indignation of Mrs. Browning.

---

[1] De Man. *Joy in Work*, p. 106.   [2] *The Town Labourer*, p. 21.
[3] Marx. *Capital* (tr. E. and C. Paul), p. 368.

> " For all day the wheels are droning, turning ;
>   Their wind comes in our faces,
> Till our hearts turn, our heads with pulses burning,
>   And the walls turn in their places :
> Turns the sky in the high window, blank and reeling,
>   Turns the long light that drops down the wall,
> Turn the black flies that crawl along the ceiling :
>   All are turning, all the day, and we with all.
> And all day the iron wheels are droning,
>   And sometimes we could pray,
> ' O ye wheels ' (breaking out in a mad moaning),
>   ' Stop ! be silent for to-day ! ' "[1]

It has often been pointed out that one of the drawbacks of certain machine conditions of labour is that the worker has to follow and obey the rhythm of the machine. Marx summed up the matter long ago in his chapter on ' Machinery and Large Scale Industry ' :—

> " In manufacture and in handicrafts, the worker uses a tool ; in the factory he serves a machine. In the former case, the movements of the instrument of labour proceed from the worker ; but in the latter, the movements of the worker are subordinate to those of the machine. In manufacture, the workers are parts of a living mechanism. In the factory, there exists a lifeless mechanism independent of them, and they are incorporated into that mechanism as its living appendages."[2]

Large-scale production has been carried further since Marx wrote the chapter in which this passage occurs, and the use of swifter, more powerful and more intricate machinery as well as the use of the continuous conveyor system, especially in mass-production processes, have increased the sense of subordination and dependence on an external power. " The machine sets the pace " is the complaint that underlies a number of reports that I have received from workers engaged in any form of

---

[1] *The Cry of the Children* (anno 1844).
[2] Marx. *Capital* (tr. E. and C. Paul), p. 451.

machine-feeding or routine operation dictated by the speed of the machine.

A 'minder' in a cotton spinning mill describes his work as follows :—

"The mule is fed by boys and the process-work of turning the partly prepared cotton sieves into yarn is controlled by the spinner who is termed the minder. . . The minder is responsible for the production of good yarn and if any complaints have to be made the minder is the person to whom they are made.

The machine dominates my work. I have to follow every movement of the mule, and as the speed increases so must I. If I leave the machine the broken threads accumulate and the mule must be stopped whilst the broken ends are pieced."

The demands of a conveyor are still more unrelenting.

A 'screen-hand' in a coal mine says :—

"Coal comes past me on an endless belt, and it is my duty to separate any dirt there may be from the coal. The belt sets the pace at which I must work. I have no feeling of power when working at the machine : on the contrary, I feel dwarfed, and I feel that the machine, instead of serving man, has become his master."

A 'putter' in a coalmine says :—

"The improvement of machinery for coal-cutting at the coal face out-distanced the improvements for getting the coal from the face to the landing-stage or flat as the miners call it. Hence, the putter could not transport the coal from the face as rapidly as the men and the machines could cut it.

"Further, the improvements for getting the coal from the landing-stage have out-distanced the putter's ability to carry it from the coal-face. The result is that the setts or wagon trains are always waiting for the putter. These factors between them contrived to make my life a hell : one machine was vomiting more than I could clean up, while the other had a larger mouth than I could fill. The outcome of this was a constant worry : I was working always at the top speed without any sense of rhythm. I often wished that all machines and the men who made them were in hell burning. Until they improve on the methods of getting coal from the coal-face I shall always regard machines in the mine as a nerve-racking, soul-crushing element."

The large-scale mass-production factory affects some workers with a depressing if not terrifying sense of their subordination. A former student of Ruskin College has given a vivid description of his own experience in his book *The Triumphant Machine.*

" I write," he says, " from an intimate knowledge of modern machine industry with its mass-production, its speeding-up and general soullessness. When I entered industry I found it a nightmare of time-recording clocks which rang with a sharp staccato clang when the cards were stamped and of numbered brass tool checks which impressed upon me that my place in the universe was C. 702, a contention which I instinctively disputed. No one had any individuality at all. The machine took hold of me with its iron fingers and worked me to the shape required. Every second had to be accounted for. As I ' clocked off ' one job, I ' clocked on ' to the next. In the department where I worked galleries rose in tiers, and at each side, from gallery to gallery, stretched a set of rails along which lumbered huge cranes which picked up solid masses of metal from the iron tables of the machines and dropped them else-where. Everything conspired to dwarf the individual ; men looked like hurrying gnomes amid the whirring wheels, while the metal groaned and shrieked in every key as it was cut and shaped. The whole works was one great machine, of which we were parts that could easily be scrapped and replaced. This drove some of the men to drink; some it made ' work beasts ' who worked and slept resignedly; others it gave the unreasoned pessimism of the hump. All suffered, even those who accepted it most placidly. For to be geared to a machine is not a human life."[1]

The writer of that is doubtless not a typical mass-production worker. The artist in him may make him more sensitive than most men to the harshness of factory life. But his capacity for self-expression enables him to put into words the kind of feeling that at any rate at times oppresses his inarticulate fellow workers, and even allowing for an element of picturesque exaggeration we are compelled to recognise that he has drawn attention to a condition of nervous strain that is a not infrequent accompaniment of mass-production machine work. ' The terror of the machine ' is intensified by the immense scale of the lay-out, the plant and the organisation behind it in modern large-scale industry. Even the size of the machine itself is an influential factor. A printer who works sometimes at ' Flat work ' and sometimes in the Rotary section writes as follows :—

" In both sections the machinery dominates you, but considerably more so in the Rotary section. This is because the Rotary machines are so much bigger and are always running at the same time. The noise is deafening. In Flat printing, the machines are run just as soon as they are ready to run. This means that more often than not some are running, and others are being ' made ready.' It can always be reckoned that half are standing still. They are not so big as Rotary machines, and so are less awesome."

But more often it is not the size of the machine itself but the size of the undertaking that exercises a depressing effect on the workers' individuality.

[1] p. 3.

Just as the size of the universe has sometimes the effect of scaring the human mind into the pitiable sense of impotence that has been called ' astronomical intimidation,' so the sheer scale of the modern factory or works may have a certain intimidating effect upon the worker's mind. In either case the mind may be unreasonably influenced by size, but the fact remains that the individual is dominated by the influence and cannot easily escape it.

And the same causes that produce a sense of littleness and inferiority in the subordinate machine worker give to those who occupy any position involving a measure of control and direction—whether over the machinery or the personnel of a works—a sense of peculiar power. And this applies both to the big machine and the big concern. The man who is engaged in operating and controlling the power unit—the dynamo or the driving machine—directing its energy and volume from a central switch board and able at a moment by pressing a button or moving a lever to accelerate or retard or arrest the movement of the machinery has a sense of wielding immense power. To a limited extent anyone who operates a machine over whose *tempo* and movement he has control feels something of that sense of enhanced power. And similarly, the person in a position of authority and control over a whole concern or even over a large department has a sense of exercising power that is pleasing to himself if not always to his colleagues or subordinates.

It is even possible that the control of machinery may for some workers compensate for their lack of control over the rest of their life and work.

" There are some machines," says an electrician, " which I enjoy manipulating. Most men are denied a controlling voice in any part of their lives, and so it is partly satisfying to one's desire for power to be able to pull a lever or a switch, and lo ! steel bends like cardboard, or shrieks off in curling blue and orange shavings : or a flat piece of steel is thrown from the 'innards' of a machine as a finished article ! "

The haulage man who is responsible for controlling the speed of the conveyors which dominate the work of the screen hand or the putter may himself enjoy a sense of power, even though he is responding to a system of signals. " I loathed sacrificing speed," one of them told me.

" I well remember," said the same man, " the feeling of pleasure tempered perhaps with apprehension when I was called upon and instructed as to control and supervision of these haulage machines : it was, I think, the feeling of power rather than the technical construction of the machine that claimed my interest."

Another miner, who was mainly engaged in working on the conveyor and filling trams with coal, contrasts the sense of rush and pressure of such work with the " feeling of considerable power " which he experienced on the rare occasions when he drove a haulage engine.

" It was almost exhilarating to find oneself able to control a train of trams, a mass of fifty or sixty tons, by a little extra pressure on the brake or an increase of the motive power. Haulage drivers of my acquaintance took considerable delight in controlling their loads."

The driver of a railway engine or a motor car is apt to experience a certain elation in his capacity to forge ahead along the track or road. An engine-driver speaks of feeling this " when travelling at speed with a big train." A chauffeur says, " I always have a feeling of elation when driving ; the speed and the hum of the engine giving an exhilarating sensation."

Agricultural workers value tractors or combine-harvesters because of their superiority over other methods of ploughing or harvesting. A worker in a Jewish agricultural colony in Palestine said to me :

" In agriculture the worker is usually the master of the machine and sets it to his pace.   I personally used to sense when working with machinery a feeling of enlarged arms and strength.   I remember when I first started the tractor and he (*sic*) pulled in the knife of the big plough deep into the earth, I wanted to cry out : ' Now, I'll tackle you, Mother Earth ! '   Before we got the tractor we had to do the preparation of the land for planting by hand-digging, using a wide hand-digger— it was a very strenuous job.

" My experience with a machine which sets the pace for the worker—the threshing machine—was a feeling of being tuned up (similar to the effect of music when you march), and of getting things done."

One frequently hears people speak of machines with which they are intimately familiar as if they were animated with a measure of life and even of personality.   The personal pronoun ' he ' in the statement just quoted is significant.   ' She ' is the more usual expression among Western speakers.   I find myself referring to the engine of my motor car in personal terms—" She's running well to-day," or " I've had some trouble in getting her to start."   A man who has worked with several kinds of machinery—grinding machines, drills and lathes, as well as electric motors—draws attention to their ' individuality':

" A man regards a machine as a power in his hands, a partner—sometimes he even gives it a personal name, as one does a ship.   He coaxes it, calling it a ' grand un ' when it runs smoothly, and ' that bastard contraption ' when something is wrong."

A Thames Conservancy river-keeper who controls a motor-boat tells me that " a long acquaintance with the boat has developed a sort of affection for it."   Among the workers whose reactions to machinery are reported by M. Henri de Man in his *Joy in Work*, many speak in terms of personal affection of both tools and machines.   He quotes a machinist who was mournful at parting from his " iron companion," a metal borer who was " particularly fond of a great drilling machine," a typist who said " I love my machine," an engine-driver who spoke affectionately of his engine as " my old horse."[1]

Many workers are possessive in their attachment to tools and machinery and jealous of anyone else who handles them. They know just how their own machine ' likes ' to be treated, the precise conditions under which it will do its best, and they distrust a stranger who does not understand ' its little ways.'

A machine has its ' moods,' and although a worker may not feel affection for it he will respect its idiosyncrasies and try to humour it.

A miner in charge of a haulage engine writes :—

" I felt that the machine was strangely human : it had to be fed and lubricated, and although I detested having to look after it and attend to its wants, its sheer responsiveness after being greased and oiled compelled me to devote a certain amount of my leisure to perform this very necessary function rather than face up to a noisy, complaining and utterly indifferent machine."

Mr. W. F. Watson, writing from thirty years' experience as a working mechanic, has described as " almost universal " the disregard by otherwise well-organised firms of small equipment such as tools and tackle. Insufficient supplies and inferior qualities of spanners, drill chucks and other tools are frequent :

" Boring bars, cans and brushes for cutting lubricant, dusting brushes for keeping the lathe free from dust and turnings, belt dressing, rope, packing for tool posts, are other ' important trivialities ' neglected by many managements. Such things are as necessary as any part of the plant."[2]

[1] *op. cit.*, p. 28–33.
[2] In *The Worker's Point of View*, p. 20.

Mr. Watson points out that " people rarely value things that do not belong to them ; still less do they value things that *partly* belong to them, unless they are placed exclusively in their charge, and it is in their interest to take care of them."[1] He describes an early and short-lived experiment in Scientific Management in which each day everything was taken out of the shops and put in the stores, and in which the workers were forbidden to grind their own tools.

" What these people failed to understand was that there is individuality in grinding a tool. A man may be quite competent to grind *his* tools to his complete satisfaction, but he cannot always grind *my* tools to suit *me*. Moreover, having adapted a tool to suit his purpose, a man values it, and likes to keep it."[2]

Mr. Watson suggests that each machine, e.g., a lathe, should have its own complete tool kit, with every article stamped with the number of the machine, and that the operator should be held responsible for the number and condition of the tools.

" It will be contended that even in such ideal conditions some workmen will continue to maltreat tools and tackle. Maybe. But not many. The knowledge that there was an adequate supply of everything, and that everything could be obtained quickly without ' scrounging ' round the shop for it ; the fact that he would be held individually responsible for its condition while it was in his possession, would cause him to value tackle ; and having a complete kit of accessories to his lathe which he must not lend (neither can he borrow anything), he would take great care of them because, for the time being, they were for his exclusive use. The periodical tool inspection would soon make the habitual maltreater recognise the advisability of mending his ways.

---

[1] *The Worker's Point of View*, p. 22.　　　　[2] *Ibid.*, p. 23.

" ' But look at the expense ! ' many employers will say, aghast at the very idea of such a bold scheme. Undoubtedly the initial cost would be heavy, but would it not be worth all the expense to remove one of the most fruitful causes of waste of time, irritation and friction between workmen ? The increased output and the enormous saving of time would soon pay for the initial cost."[1]

The worker may feel fear or hatred for the machine, either because it dominates his work, or because it is dangerous to life and limb. A worker at a drilling machine tells me that he has witnessed several accidents, in two of which his father was a victim. On one occasion he saw his father severely cut and bruised by a drilling machine in which his overall jacket got entangled, and on another he saw his leg crushed and broken by the fall of a heavy steel plate which had slipped from the chain of an overhead crane.

" I have never been very partial to machinery and after the second incident I grew to dislike it even more intensely. There seemed to be something relentless about it."

If some workers feel a sense of personal affection or dislike for the machines which they operate, others, even though exercising a measure of control, feel the machine an alien and impersonal thing. This will be more likely to be the reaction of those who have little to do beyond controlling the running of the machine. A machine assistant working at a newspaper press describes his work as a ' button-hand.'

" The button-hand starts up the machine by pressing a button, and keeps it going until the reel, or reels of paper are unwound from the spindles. Normally this takes about half an hour, after which a few minutes would elapse for fresh ones to be joined up, and then off

[1] *The Worker's Point of View*, p. 26.

G

would go the machine again, devouring in its jaws of steel miles and miles of paper.

" If the paper breaks, the operator must instantly apply the stop button, or the loose end will wind itself round somewhere, with serious results.

" Whilst the machine is running his job is to watch the paper travelling through the cylinders, and to make sure that this is continued without mishap. Twisting and curling, it flies through at a tremendous pace, and if ever you have tried watching a swiftly moving object, you can appreciate how trying this can be for the eyes. When I am doing this I have great difficulty in keeping them open especially during the night. I watch the clock, and if the reel is dressed, I conjecture how much remains before it will be unwound.

" Sometimes I look forward to a wreckage to relieve the monotony, for it may be some time then before the machine is ready again to run at its 30,000 revolutions per hour."

This illustration shows that the work of the machine-*minder* may be as monotonous as that of the machine-*feeder* and give no more scope for individuality or initiative. A telegraph operator describes her work at a teleprinter—a multiplex direct printing telegraph mechanism worked by local batteries. The actual manual work is performed by touch-type typing.

" I do not like operating," she says, " though I have no lively antipathy to it. I have a distant admiration for and appreciation of the instrument as a technical achievement but cannot identify myself with it in any way. There is certainly some pleasure in its quick disposal of work, but on the other hand there is not the slightest element of craftsmanship. With earlier and less ambitious (and much slower) types of instrument and particularly the Morse telegraph instrument, an operator could develop an individual and characteristic style, which was both stimulating and pleasurable. . . . With the modern instrument . . . . there is practically no scope for originality and personality in operating."

The reports of their reactions to machinery which various types of machine-worker have given suggest two considerations of importance.

(1) Machinery over whose speed and rhythm the worker has no control, machinery that 'sets the pace' and dominates the worker's operation and its rate, is liable to produce a sense of strain and tension accompanied by feelings either of lively resentment or of sullen acquiescence. Machine-feeding of a more or less automatic kind is therefore likely to involve 'human costs' which are not always taken into account, and which, even if they do not contribute to the 'business costs of industrial inefficiency'[1] (in calculable items of lost time, quantity and quality of output, accidents, ill-health, and labour turnover) nevertheless represent a waste of human energy and capacity.

" It is often said that the man who feeds a machine tends to become as automatic as the machine itself. This, however, is but a half-truth. If the tender could become as automatic as the machine he tended, if he could completely mechanise a little section of his faculties, it might go easier with him. But the main trend of life in the man fights against the mechanising tendency of the work, and the struggle entails a heavy cost. For his machine imposes a repetition of the same muscular and nervous action upon a being whose muscles and nervous resources are continually changing. The machine, fed constantly with the same supply of fuel, geared up to a single constant pace of movement, forced by unchanging structure to the performance of the same operation, friction and error reduced to an

[1] Sargent Florence. *Economics of Fatigue and Unrest*, ch. v.

almost negligible minimum, works through the longest day with a uniform expenditure of power. The machine-tender is an organism, fed at somewhat irregular intervals with different amounts and sorts of food, the assimilation of which is also discontinuous, and incapable of maintaining intact and constant in its quality the muscular and nervous tissue and accompanying contractions which constitute the physical supply of ' work.' This organism has also many other structures and functions, physical and mental, whose activities and needs get in the way of the automatic activity of machine-tending. Thus the worker cannot succeed in becoming altogether a machine-tending automaton. He will not always exactly repeat himself, and his attempt to do so involves two sets of organic costs or wastes, due to the fact that, *though his labour tries to make him a specialised mechanism, he remains a generalised organism.*"[1]

It is the mechanical work that involves these human costs which requires to be eliminated, and the best way to demechanise work that is dehumanising may well be to mechanise it still further.[2] A little machine has recently been invented which automatically adjusts a washer to a screw—with a saving of time, room, labour, and especially monotony. Many more such devices may be expected. " The advance of technical invention will make it possible in the end to transform all mechanised work into supervision," prophesied Walther Rathenau.[3] But he admits that it will be a long process, and in the meantime advocates an ' interchange of labour ' between mechanical and other forms of employment, for example, between intellectual and mechanical employment ; or, we might add, between indoor and outdoor employment.

But a great part of the strain of repetitive machine-

---

[1] J. A. Hobson. *Work and Wealth*, p. 62. (The italics are his.)
[2] De Man. *Joy in Work*, p. 112.
[3] *The New Society*, p. 110.

tending is due not to the mere repetition of movements but to the ' speeding-up ' which is imposed on the workers by those who control the speed of the machines and the rate of production. The continuous flow system of necessity involves a fairly uniform rate over which the workers or their supervisors may have some control by signalling apparatus, but which is likely to be kept at a maximum. But there are other forms of machine-work in which it is possible to utilise either a system of centralised controls or a system of separate motors for each engine, and here there are definite advantages from the point of view of the human factor in the latter system. For recent physiological studies indicate that different individuals have a different innate or natural rhythm or *tempo*, and that this will dictate an optimum working rhythm. Professor Cathcart makes an interesting observation on this point.

" If this belief " (he says) " in the existence of individual rhythms and rates of working is correct then the whole system of the average workshop organisation with its centralised power-plant, and the distribution of power throughout the workshop is fundamentally wrong. . . . Instead of working at his optimum rhythm and rate the average man has to-day the inexorable rhythm of power-driven machinery. I have been informed by one employer of labour that since he introduced a series of electric motors, one attached to each machine and directly under the control of the worker, the quality of the work and the output have increased. He also informed me that very few of the machines run at the same rate, and moreover that the speed varied from day to day with individuals."[1]

The Industrial Fatigue Research Board have published a report dealing with various types of machinery in use, which shews that in the design of the machines :

[1] *The Human Factor in Industry*, p. 29.

" Little or no attention has been devoted to the human being who is responsible for working the machine. Many of these machines involve an unnecessary amount of stooping and reaching on the part of the operative, the height of the parts has not been adjusted to meet the worker, pedals are placed in difficult positions or require an undue amount of pressure to operate, the operative may receive a severe shock owing to sudden acceleration towards the end of travel succeeded by an equally sudden check, other machines are real sources of danger to the worker either because the moving parts are in close proximity to the heads or the limbs of the operative or because the illumination of the machine is defective."[1]

The Board has been co-operating with the Department of Industrial and Scientific Research in an enquiry into the design of machines from this standpoint.[2]

(2) Machinery over whose speed and rhythm and working operations the worker exercises control is likely to give him a sense of enhanced power, interest and responsibility in proportion as the machine is his partner and not merely either his master or his slave.

The machine-*minder* may be in control of the machine, but he is merely doing things *to* it and not doing things *with* it. Consequently he is not necessarily in any happier or more interesting relation to the machine than the machine-*feeder* who feels that the machine is doing things to or with him. But the man who is doing or making something with the help of a machine feels that he is working *with* the machine in a partnership that is all the pleasanter because he remains the senior partner. Consequently, we find that the worker who is driving a machine, and not merely driving but directing its operations, usually enjoys machine-work more than the

---

[1] Cathcart. *op. cit.*, p. 74.
[2] Myers. *Industrial Psychology in Great Britain*, p. 17.

worker who is either feeding or minding a machine which is otherwise operating independently. Again, the worker who is concerned in designing, ' doctoring ' or repairing machinery finds scope for skill and ingenuity and personal expression. Of such work a correspondent writes :

" His relationship to the machine is not unlike that of a doctor to his patient. His trained ear can often detect coming trouble and his clear insight enables him to administer treatment which removes the cause of the trouble. Knowing his machine through and through, a pride and satisfaction in, and perhaps a feeling of responsibility for, the finished article, the product of his machine, also his complete knowledge of the mechanical processes and his artistic sense may enable him to make such adjustments in his machine as will enable it to produce a finer, lovelier article, one which, although mass-produced, has an appeal to our ' æsthetic sense.' "

With these conditions in mind, we may turn to the question how far machine-work can offer interest and satisfaction to the worker.

CHAPTER IX

M. HENRI DE MAN in his book, *Der Kampf um die Arbeits-freude* (translated into English under the title *Joy in Work*), analysed the factors that go to make work satisfying to the worker and the hindrances and inhibitions arising from the technical conditions of the work or the social conditions of the worker. Among the primary factors that make for joy in work he distinguishes the impulses connected with activity, play, constructiveness, curiosity, self-assertion, possessiveness and combativeness. To these he adds as accessory factors gregariousness, mastery and subordination, æsthetic gratification, self-interest, social advantage, and finally, a sense of social obligation.

Among the technical hindrances to satisfaction he distinguishes detail process work, repetitive work, fatigue, and bad workshop conditions, such as defective ventilation or sanitation, danger, noise, bad lighting, dirt and ugliness.

To these he adds the hindrances arising from unsatisfactory conditions of labour, such as long hours, unjust wage systems, speeding up, and repressive discipline ; and the hindrances arising from unsatisfactory conditions outside the workshop, such as insecurity of employment and therefore of livelihood, inferior social status, and the conventional disparagement of ' manual ' labour.

The conclusion to which he comes is a hopeful one, because he finds reason to believe that " the acceptance of technical advance need not involve the renunciation of joy in work."[1]   He bases his belief on the evidence which

---

[1] *Joy in Work*, p. 220.

he derived from a collection of seventy-eight autobiographical reports supplied by wage workers and salaried employees of both sexes from various parts of Germany, who were students at the Labour College attached to the University of Frankfurt in the years 1924–1926. Although the students in question were for the most part bitter opponents of Capitalism and influenced by the Marxian outlook which prevails throughout the German working-class movement, their personal attitude toward their work appears to have been much less influenced by their political opinions than might have been expected.

" Fifty-seven per cent. of them declare that they find joy in their work, and only nineteen per cent. that a feeling of distaste for work predominates."[1]

It is not surprising to find that :

" The reports shew that joy in work increases with an increase in the skill requisite for the occupation. Of the unskilled workers who reported to me, only eleven per cent. say that joy in work predominates over distaste for work ; of the semi-skilled workers, forty-four per cent. tell me this ; and of the skilled workers, sixty-seven per cent. . . . . Pride in their own skill, which breathes through the reports of all the skilled workers, is amazingly strong."[2]

Among the skilled workers, handicraftsmen in the older sense (builders, carpenters and the like) formed only a minority. The majority were printers and compositors, engineers, machinists, engine-drivers, and so on.

Although M. de Man's book is of the highest interest and importance, and the extracts from the personal statements of his students are exceedingly illuminating, I am doubtful if the summary statement that fifty-seven per cent. found joy in their work and only nineteen per cent. a predominating distaste for it is of much value. Everything turns on the meaning that each individual

[1] *Joy in Work*, p. 218.   [2] *Ibid.*, p. 85.

attaches to terms like 'joy' and 'distaste.' It is perhaps unfortunate that the term *Arbeitsfreude* has been translated as 'Joy in Work,' for the word 'joy' in English commonly stands for an elated if not ecstatic condition, and 'enjoyment' or 'satisfaction' comes nearer to what was probably intended. But even with this modification, it is evident that expressions like satisfaction or liking and dissatisfaction or distaste are used to describe so great a range of feelings as to be very nearly meaningless save as broad distinctions. My own enquiries in the year 1932 among some fifty workers of both sexes drawn from very different occupations and localities leave me unable to make any general statement. What I aimed at discovering about the sense of satisfaction in their work was at what points in it they were liable to find most interest and enjoyment; at what points they became tired or bored; and what were the conditions making for satisfaction or dissatisfaction. On these questions it may be of interest to record some of the replies.

The workers who expressed themselves as feeling little or no interest or satisfaction in their work were mostly performing semi-skilled 'feeding' operations—three of them in connection with the haulage system in coal mines, and two of them in mass-production factory work. One of them is a woman clerical officer in the Civil Service who works with posting and balancing machines.

The workers on the other hand who spoke of some degree of interest and satisfaction found it in those points in their work in which one or other of the following appeared :

> (a) craftsmanship.
> (b) technical ingenuity.
> (c) 'making a good job of it.'
> (d) interest in the outcome.
> (e) human contacts.
> (f) responsibility.

(a) *Craftsmanship*, in the older sense, was represented by agriculture, carpentry, and building work. The satisfaction of the agricultural worker, both in the varied skills of his calling and in the changing face of nature and the processes of growth, is counteracted by the low standard of life. " It doesn't matter how hard one works no more return is forthcoming," says one. Another says that he likes agricultural work, and would only prefer another occupation on economic grounds. Apart from this drawback, the work and its natural conditions provide a unique opportunity for satisfactions that fulfil some of the most deeply-rooted human needs. It is significant that in a group of Ruskin College students who were consulted twenty years ago (not indeed by any thorough method of enquiry) only the agricultural labourer among them expressed himself as deriving pleasure from his work.[1]

A joiner employed in the maintenance joinery department of a large mass-production factory finds his work enjoyable :

" Joinery is extremely interesting with its geometrical problems and necessity for accuracy, and it is satisfying to conquer these problems and to be able to say, ' Well, I have made a real good job of that,' and ' with these hands and this brain have I created usefulness and beauty.' "

The same man adds a scathing comment on the mass-production work of the manufacturing departments of the firm in which he is employed, and its effects on the workers. " Little wonder they become nervous wrecks pitiful to watch," he says, and he hints at madness, deformity and early death among their ranks. This is no doubt an extravagant indictment, but I cite it because it reveals the indignation and hostility which the mass-production system excites in the craftsman.

[1] Wallas. *The Great Society*, p. 345.

A man who has had a varied experience, including that of a builder's labourer, prefers the latter to any machine work except that of a cinema operator.

" I have found that men were happier and more satisfied in trades where machinery had not entered to a large extent. This was noticeable in the building trade, and I much preferred this work myself, although being clumsy in some ways I did not get on so well."

(b) *Technical ingenuity.* All those of my informants who had some degree of mechanical training and whose work involved either the use of machinery for making things or the supervision, adjustment and repair of machines, found considerable interest in their work. Electricians, engineers and machinists got the most enjoyment from their work, especially when it called for the exercise of ingenuity.

An electrician writes :

" I like the type of complex machine and complex job where it is necessary to scheme and adjust—the job to try one's wits, and the machine to help one to solve the problem. . . . A big machine shop is always yielding problems of improved or new usage, or of repair, which give joy and pride to the craft engineer, and breed a knowledge of and love for his machines. . . . I feel interest in a job . . . out of which I can wring a measure of self-esteem, one which calls for general knowledge and one which maybe someone else has given up as hopeless (particularly if he was one of my superiors). . . . A new device, or a new way of using an old tool gives particular satisfaction, especially if one sees one's mates adopt one's ' invention.' "

An engine-fitter and turner says :

" I have worked all kinds of machinery, including lathes, milling machines, slotting machines, planing machines, and bevel and helical gear cutting machines.

. . . Machine work varies. The greater the degree of accuracy required, the more individual the job, the greater the interest I feel. In such a job as cutting helical gearing, great care is necessary, and there is definite satisfaction to be obtained in completing such work. . . . I have been given a great deal of freedom with regard to the method of doing work, and have found satisfaction in overcoming difficulties and in setting up jobs, or making special jigs for awkward processes."

Another turner writes :

" I am most interested when engaged on a job where it is odds on my scrapping it (on my having to scrap it), and most satisfied when the foreman says, ' I didn't think you would manage it.' "

Textile workers engaged in supervising or minding spinning machines speak of finding the greatest interest when the work calls for alterations, adjustments or repairs.

Two men, who have had a succession of varied jobs, speak of finding their greatest interest and satisfaction in the cinema industry—one as sound-recording cameraman in a film studio and the other as cinematograph operator. The former, when asked at what points in his work he had found interest and satisfaction, replied : " At every point in the film trade, at none in the factory." (He had been a packer in an electrical factory.)

" I enjoyed working a sound-camera. . . . I was always interested because, sound-recording being in little more than an experimental stage, technical changes were being made almost every day. There was nearly always some new gadget to keep an eye on, and it was interesting to see whether the experiments would be successful or not."

In non-mechanical occupations the situation that calls for the exercise of ingenuity is also the high point of interest.

An accountant's clerk writes :

" Of actual accountancy I must say that I got small satisfaction out of it. . . . What I did enjoy was tracking down obscure points in law and spending the morning in a library finding cases. I enjoyed, moreover, dictating letters and drafting reports, attending board meetings or shareholders' meetings where some element of criticism might be expected. The desire to show what the accounts meant, to explore with a Board the chances of persuading the Inland Revenue people to agree to certain courses—these were the parts of the work I most enjoyed. But the creation of a balance sheet or the balancing of accounts (over which I have known men to grow really enthusiastic) never really interested me. On the other hand I have noticed that colleagues have grown wearied and completely careless when an undiscovered error has eluded us for days. I rarely got tired of hunting for discrepancies—largely because I never did the routine work over again but preferred to analyse the books, balance first this ledger and then that, and so always had the consciousness that I was narrowing towards the source of error."

It is significant that this man has developed a great liking for law, although it alternated with journalism and teaching in his ambitions, and is now reading for a law degree. It is also of interest that a pure chance determined that he should become an accountant's clerk and not a solicitor's clerk.

(c) ' *Making a good job of it.*' We have already seen the part that good workmanship plays in the satisfaction of both the older type of craftsman and the modern type of engineer. But in all occupations the feeling of turning out some piece of work successfully and well affords the highest degree of satisfaction. The electrician who says, " I feel satisfied when I can look the job over and say, ' There, you miserable old devil, find fault with *that* if you can,' " is matched by the railway-engine fireman who likes " getting the best results from the least effort and the least amount of coal," and " planning work scientifically for this end," or by the shop-assistant who likes dressing a window effectively or making a ' good sale.'

A labourer writes :

" I feel interest in the work of going to a road without pavements and unlaid, and transforming this into a neat and finished job, improving its appearance and utility.   I find more interest in the job itself when it is nearing completion and its ugliness is disappearing."

(d) *Interest in the outcome.*   One of the most frequent objections to modern methods of production with their subdivided operations is that the worker is unable to see or even sometimes to imagine the final product of his work.   This is probably less true of the mass-production factory in which the product takes gradual shape as it passes through a series of stages by a continuous ' flow ' than of the works in which raw material is being worked up into a semi-finished product for the supply of manu-facturing industries.   A worker in the rolling mill at a steelworks says :

" I think I would have gained more satisfaction if I could have seen my labour contribute definitely to making something more immediately useful.   It takes some imagination to picture the ultimate uses to which stacks of steel bars can be applied, though I frequently amused myself by converting them in imagination into fruit cans, motor-car bodies, etc."

A colliery haulage engineman writes :

" The work seemed futile because one could not see that the ultimate purpose was being fulfilled—welfare. I felt rushed to do, and serve all this mechanism, just

for the mechanism's sake.   Produce, produce, produce !
for what ?   No one seemed interested in the question."

Even when the product and the use to which it will
be put is known, it may not inspire interest in the worker.
A smith's striker in a railway works says :

> " There were times when I felt a kind of savage
> impotence, there seemed to be no point in the work,
> it did not lead anywhere.   The whole process was
> devoid of ultimate significance.   Recognition of the
> fact that I was performing a necessary process in the
> construction of a railway engine did not provide me
> with any source of satisfaction."

Those workers, on the other hand, who see the finished
fruit of their work derive a peculiar satisfaction.   Of
the older crafts, agriculture and horticulture yield this
in the fullest degree.   A worker who has had experience
of both farm-work and gardening speaks of his satisfaction " in seeing the crops spring up that I have been
responsible for sowing, and in the production of a lovely
plant or flower."   The sense of personal achievement is
here completed by the visible result.

You not only make a good job of it but you see it
through and see its final yield.   Mr. Street's rhapsody on
ploughing in *Farmer's Glory* vividly communicates this
feeling.   He broke up a hundred and sixty acres of
virgin prairie in Manitoba.

> " I do not remember when I have been more satisfied
> with my lot ;   even to-day the memory of that job gives
> me great pleasure.   In thinking about it now it has
> come upon me with rather an unpleasant shock, that
> as far as I can see, I have ploughed my last furrow,
> as my present farm in England is now all grass, and
> I do not possess any plough.   This thought saddens
> me, for ploughing is the king of jobs.   In itself it is
> all-sufficing and soul-satisfying."[1]

[1] *Farmer's Glory*, p. 141.

He describes the " detached satisfaction " with which he noted " the perfect furrow, which falls away on your right in an infinite ribbon." On that quarter-section of land in North West Manitoba he feels that he has written his signature, " a signature of which I shall never be ashamed."[1]

If the machine-worker has a less direct and personal sense of individual achievement, of " mixing his labour " with the medium in which he works, he may yet have the sense of contributing to some splendid purpose. An electrician describes " a feeling regarding machines which many imaginative workers have, but which few of them would admit—a feeling of romance," and he goes on :

" We have the idea that we are pygmies who hold a race of giants in thrall—such elemental giants as steam, steel, water and electricity, whom we unite and harness to do our bidding. Some workers feel the romance, the drama, the control over destiny, as they switch on the giant presses, or teem the golden cascades of molten steel. I remember a worker in a modern mechanised bakery (where I had been installing some motors). He became almost lyrical in appreciation of the romance of his task. Golden grain gleaned from the farthest corners of the earth gathered into his room, and after being subjected to a series of operations in which hardly a hand came near, it was sent out to the people as bread. I get this feeling of romance as I watch a printing press. Firstly, my mind is filled with interest from a technical point of view, but that gives place to romance as imagination begins to play. For as the press reels off knowledge to the millions who may read the books, it appears to be a vast cornucopia, pouring out unlimited mental food, and the little inky, oily men who attend this bounty are always a source of

---

[1] *Farmer's Glory*, p. 144.

H

interest to me, and I am pleased when I find one who sees his task in the same light as I do."

Imagination of this kind is perhaps rare, but the passage suggests the possibilities of interesting workers, through school and workshop training, in the whole process and purpose of an industry. It suggests also the importance, if interest in work is to be enlisted, of being able to justify the job as contributing to some socially valuable purpose.

The same man writes :

" I feel particularly interested and satisfied if the job is of social value. If I thought that anything was for armament work I felt as Judas must have felt when he drew *his* wages. . . . But when I come out of some working-class slum in which I have left my work, then I am proud and satisfied in a certain measure. I find it dark and often dirty. I should like to pull it down. But I go in, and like a missionary (but more effectively) 'spread light in dark places' with electricity."

In the light of these considerations it would appear that the question of the quality of workmanship and quality of goods produced is of importance from the point of view of the producer as well as that of the consumer. No man can be satisfied in his work if he is neither provided with good material nor encouraged to make a good article. Contrast the report of a textile-worker that he gets most satisfaction " when a new quality of yarn is introduced of good quality " in the knowledge that " something sound and substantial will result," with this account of a mill-owner quoted by Mr. Stuart Chase.

" The commodities which issue from his mill are but counters in a purely financial transaction. He is indifferent to their quality so long as they fulfil their commercial function, and the limit of their badness is the limit of the consumer's tolerance—which is not easily reached, since the purchaser can buy only that which is offered for sale."[1]

We have already drawn attention to the loss of quality and durability in modern manufactured goods.[2] " The business man," says Mr. Chase, " often cannot tolerate durability, because of the brake it puts upon sales." And whether or no the worker may complain, the machine does not. " A craftsman cannot afford to waste good work on bad material, but all materials look alike to the machine."[3]

If there is waste of goods on account of bad material, there is also waste of work on account of speeding-up. A girl who took a job in a mass-production wireless and gramophone factory, after describing the monotony even of comparatively skilled operations, goes on to say :

" Very soon the girls take only as much interest in their work as is required to make it pass muster. Nor is this by any means their own fault. Speed is considered the first essential in factory work—not efficiency. From the point of view of the time-sheet it is better to turn out 100 coils, half of which later prove useless, than 70 perfect ones in the same time."[4]

(e) *Human contacts.* There are many workers who find compensation for the uninteresting and unsatisfactory character of their actual work in the opportunities it affords for intercourse with fellow workers. They would rather work at a monotonous occupation in company with others than at a more intrinsically interesting one alone. The village youth who prefers to seek an occupation in the town rather than to stay on the land, or the city girl who prefers to go into a factory rather than to enter domestic service, are attracted partly by the higher standard of life, but partly no doubt by the opportunity

[1] *Men and Machines*, p. 229.
[2] *Supra*, p. 34.   [3] *op. cit.*, p. 229.
[4] *What Factory Work Feels Like* (*The Friend*, Sept. 23rd, 1932).

of living and working alongside a number of others. No doubt, the gregarious tendency finds its natural expression in smaller groupings rather than in crowds, and the craving for city life and crowd conditions is an unhealthy symptom, but the fact remains that many people are attracted for various reasons to occupations in which they are brought into contact with numbers of their fellows. Mass-production may thus meet the requirements—healthy or unhealthy—of mass-consciousness and mass-suggestion. That factory workers become to a large extent ' conditioned ' to living and moving in the mass is shewn by their preference for crowded holiday resorts. Doubtless other factors, the facilities of transport, the attraction of the ' pleasure-beach,' with its mechanised amusements, the ' anonymity ' of the individual in the crowd, and the inertia which clings to the familiar routine and evades the task of making new choices and decisions and planning the means to their accomplishment, account for the popularity of Blackpool or of Margate.

But crowd conditions do not satisfy the demands of personal friendship and affection, and just as the city suburb is notorious for its lack of neighbourliness, so the large-scale factory makes for acquaintance rather than for intimacy.

An electrician writes :

" At my job as a wireman, I often had associates with whom I could talk freely and at length. I found it of great value, both as a means of developing my powers of expression and as a means of making the hours fly faster—with no detriment to the quality though sometimes to the speed of work. The foreman would suggest that we talk after working hours but it was not usual for us to meet after working hours except upon Branch night. For strange to say, there does not appear to be a great number of people who have their workmates as bosom friends after the 'buzzer' has gone. It would appear that such associates were too reminiscent of 'work' to be pleasant company, and so friends were found from other trades and in other environments, perhaps through the medium of a sports club or a church or a political party."

Miners, by reason of their isolation in certain areas apart from other industries, are largely confined to their own circle, but here again they do not necessarily find their most intimate friends among their immediate workmates. But the miner who is working at a point remote from his fellows will welcome the more eagerly the opportunity of an exchange of conversation. One of them tells me :

" The only interest and satisfaction I found in the work was in meeting and talking to the men whom I met during the day. Visits from firemen or a fitter were anticipated with interest and people were always willing to leave their work to go in search of some person or stores."

Another miner who sees very few people throughout the shift says :

" Lack of opportunity to be interested in one's work-mates—even if interests are not similar—tends to create an unsocial attitude of mind. I tended to find pleasure in the isolation and the opportunities it afforded for thinking. This is not appreciated until one does public work, or social activity ; and years of comparative isolation then mean lack of understanding and appreciation of one's fellows' outlook."

The variety of human contacts in the film trade is one of its attractions, and a sound-recording camera-man writes of his job :—

"I like it because the work is never monotonous—

every picture means different people, different conditions and a different atmosphere. There is too a different feeling between the heads of departments and the workers—a feeling of friendliness which one does not usually find in other trades. In most trades, and particularly in factories, the foreman's most important function appears to be to grumble at anything and everything, but in the film trade there is far more tolerance and leniency towards mistakes."

In the non-mechanical operations, the shop assistant finds interest in the observations of the different kinds of customer, and a telegraph operator who finds little or no satisfaction in operating or sorting duties, speaks of finding " a good deal of pleasure in counter work or any work involving direct connexion with the public."

This also serves to give a sense of the social purpose and value of the work.

" It is only then," she adds, " that I realise that the work as a whole is a public service. And in this work, within the limits set by a multitudinous collection of rules, it is possible to introduce a definite element of personality and to find a real interest and satisfaction."

(f) *Responsibility.* Whether it be true, as Mr. Ford and others have contended, that a majority of workers prefer to be relieved from responsibility and ask nothing better than to be given their orders and to go ahead, there are certainly a large number of workers who find the highest satisfaction in their work through the exercise of responsibility, and probably a still larger number who feel cramped and repressed because they can find no scope in their work for personal expression and responsible control. It is probable that the desire for responsibility depends not only upon temperament and character but upon age, and I believe that many people as they reach the thirties hanker after more responsible work, failing which they settle down with reluctant acquiescence ranging from resentment to resignation. It is significant that the majority of those whom I have questioned are between 25 and 35 years of age, and that nearly all express themselves as eager for more responsible work than that to which they are accustomed. There are other factors that enter in. Most of them are adult students who have not only given up a considerable part of their leisure for some years to serious study but have been selected by competitive examination for scholarships to Ruskin College, and who are doubtless by disposition and by the character of their interests less adapted to the ordinary routine of industrial work than their fellows.

Moreover, those of my informants who are not students are men and women who are sufficiently interested and articulate to be willing to answer my questions. None the less, making every allowance for the restricted number and unrepresentative character of my group of informants, I believe that their age in life largely accounts for their strong feeling about the lack of responsible control in their accustomed work and for their ambitions for work of a more responsible character. I do not of course forget that more responsible work is usually work that carries higher pay and greater prestige ; these indeed may often be the most attractive features of the more responsible positions. But the fact remains that the worker who has behind him many years of experience and knowledge of his trade, and who finds himself precluded from any opportunity of effecting improvements in the work or exercising control over its conditions, is liable to become restless and dissatisfied unless he succumbs to a resigned indifference.[1]

[1] For a further discussion of the worker's desire for a share in control of management, see chapter XI.

CHAPTER X

MOTIVES TO WORK

WE saw, in discussing monotony and boredom,[1] that emotional factors are of the first importance as an impetus to effort, and that the presence or absence of interest makes a profound difference both to the quantity and quality of work. We have also seen some of the conditions that make for the interest and satisfaction of the worker. Where interest and zest are awakened, the strain of labour is correspondingly lessened. Men will work with immense energy for prolonged periods under the stimulus of human interests—whether intrinsic interests, like those of a craft or intellectual pursuit, or extrinsic interests like meeting an urgent personal or social need. It is not the least serious defect of modern industry that it fails, for so large a proportion of the workers engaged in it, to enlist the interests and motives that are conducive to good workmanship. The intrinsic interest of work is apt to be slight save in the more creative or constructive occupations or parts of an occupation, and its place cannot be filled by the merely external stimulus of want. This makes the more important the enlistment of fresh motives which will engage the interest of the whole man. For the fact is that the spring of human interest has gone out of a great part of industry to-day. Mr. Tawney in his *Acquisitive Society* discerns the familiar symptoms of economic collapse in the " failure of customary stimuli to evoke their customary response in human effort."[2] Mr. and Mrs. Sidney Webb trace " the decay of capitalist civilisation " to the moral failure of

____

[1] *Supra*, p. 72, *ff.*   [2] p. 173.

capitalism as seen in its reliance on a " socially injurious and even dangerous stimulus to activity "—the motive of gain—which is " not one by which human actions can safely be inspired."[1]

It becomes therefore important to examine the incentives to work that are at present relied upon and to ask if there are other motives which are capable of being brought into play or fostered more successfully. Motives, in industry as in other spheres of human conduct, are usually many and mixed rather than single or simple, and unwittingly rather than consciously pursued.

" The incentives operative in each person's daily work are both numerous and fluctuating in intensity. Many are operative in the background of consciousness and are seldom recognised as exerting any influence. Some seem dominant during certain periods, while in different circumstances entirely new influences operate."[2]

In singling out certain motives for discussion, therefore, we are not assuming that they operate constantly, consciously or in isolation.

Want. The original and primitive stimulus to labour as distinct from play activity is the pressure of sheer physical appetite and elementary need. Food to satisfy physical hunger, clothing and shelter for protection against the elements, are requirements that call for some measure of human effort in every form of society. In the most primitive communities then, requirements are satisfied by spells of labour in the hunting of prey or the construction of rude shelters in which the members of the clan or tribe co-operate. Wants are few and simple, and the time not occupied in such employment may be given to the adornment of the shelter, the person or the tools. The clothing of the person in temperate and warm

---

[1] *The Decay of Capitalist Civilisation*, p. 170.
[2] Miles. *The Problem of Incentives in Industry*, p. 2.

climates is a question of decoration rather than protection. The increase in the number of men's wants has led to the employment of the greater part of a man's life in some productive occupation. The primary aim of such work is the making of a livelihood, and the character of modern industry with its dependence on a ' reserve ' of unemployed labour and its frequent disturbance by irregularity of demand makes both the occupation itself and the livelihood to which it ministers undesirably precarious.

Fear. It is assumed by some defenders of the existing order or disorder that this uncertainty and insecurity is a necessary stimulus to effort, but they ignore the fact that satisfactory work is never performed under the shadow of fear or anxiety. To rely on the fear of starvation or destitution as a stimulus to work is indeed both physiologically and psychologically mistaken.

> " The assumption that the stimulus of imminent personal want is either the only spur or a sufficient spur to productive effort is a relic of a crude psychology which has little warrant either in past history or in present experience."[1]

Fear, indeed, whether of actual want or of a decline in the standard of life, is a clumsy and unreliable motive for sound, efficient and continuous work.

Nor is the fear of disciplinary measures or penalties an incentive to good work, however effective it may be as a negative deterrent from mere idleness. An American Labour Manager writes as follows :—

> " I am convinced that the greatest single hamper upon production is fear, whether in the mind of the employer or employee. Too often in the past and even in the present, fear has been made the main whip to production. But fear is a very unstable and incalculable stimulus to motive. . . . It may produce

[1] Tawney. *The Acquisitive Society*, p. 199.

high spurts of production; but it is more likely to cause a drop in production."

Competition, again, if understood as a personal contest between two or more men or groups, as to which shall have or maintain a position (as distinguished from *emulation* in which they vie as to which shall turn out the best quality of work) is a stimulus under which a man may work energetically, it is true, but not to the best satisfaction either of himself or of the community. The danger instincts in fact, alike of fear and pugnacity, are negative and secondary responses which are not reliable as prime motives of human endeavour; they are formed and evolved to meet obstruction rather than to achieve construction. And in fact they break out the more readily, and often in perverse forms, when other and more primary and central impulses are thwarted or repressed. We may perhaps see in the prevalence of alcoholism and gambling on the one hand, and in the readiness for war or revolution on the other, the symptoms of an unsatisfied human nature which is baulked of its natural expression and revolts against the unnatural and repressive conditions of modern life and labour. Industrial *unrest* is indeed not merely a negative gesture of revolt but a significant and hopeful evidence of positive demands of men and women that are at present unfulfilled.

Cupidity. And it is the more significant that this unrest is not pacified or at least finally allayed by the mere appeal to men's cupidity. It is true that high wages, piece-work payment, premium bonus systems, etc., may be very powerful inducements to regularity of work and quantity of output. None the less, it is doubtful if the mere appeal to the motive of gain can secure the best work, especially in point of quality, which demands an interest and devotion that the merely profit-seeking are not prepared to give. And it is equally doubtful if the appeal to acquisitiveness can provide a substitute for the satisfaction of the desire for freedom and self-expression.   Again and again men have shewn themselves unwilling to buy security or even affluence at the cost of liberty.

Yet it is the motive of gain and the offer of financial incentives that are most often relied upon as a stimulus to increased output.   And it cannot be denied that piece rates and bonus systems do succeed in securing certain standards of quantity if not of quality.   The systems in use vary greatly in character and effectiveness. The principle of the bonus system is that the worker shall be guaranteed a minimum rate irrespective of output, but that he shall benefit by additional efforts that enable him to do a task in less than the standard time.   To secure a fair adjustment of the pay time-studies are made and standards determined to express the average time taken by the worker on the task.

But whether the adjustment is really fair, or is felt to be fair, is another matter.   Some are so complicated that the worker cannot understand them and is consequently suspicious.   Others are unfair because the initial standard is too high, or because the rate is cut from time to time without reason or explanation.   One of the complaints against 'Taylorism' was that "the standard was intentionally set so high that only about 10 per cent. of the workers could exceed it,"[1] and that the 'high-priced' men were 'driven,' and the less efficient driven out.   Less ruthless methods have since been adopted both in America and Great Britain, including 'group bonus' systems that make for a less individualistic attitude to work, and encourage co-operative effort in the shop.   But here too, there are difficulties.

"When a group bonus system is instituted, it is necessary to take care that the groups are not too large

---

[1] Miles.   *op. cit.*, p. 11.

and to see that the workers in them are of similar efficiency. A man will willingly do extra work to maintain the standard and to ' help out ' his mate if he is temporarily ' off colour,' but he will not carry an idle or inefficient worker on his back indefinitely."[1]

One of the most satisfactory systems is the Priestman scheme, under which the whole of the workers in the firm participate in the bonus in proportion to their salaries or wages ; and this has the merit of giving an impetus to co-operative effort on the part of all the sections, administrative, clerical, technical and operative. Profit-sharing and co-partnership schemes have also been devised to give to all the employees in a firm a direct interest in the firm's success ; but these have disadvantages that have not been overcome. They are unpopular with organised Labour, they tie up the worker's savings in a restricted and possibly precarious form of investment which he cannot afford to risk, and in times of industrial depression " the profits shared may be negligible and quite useless as an incentive."

" In the highly competitive industries the surplus is often so small and is distributed at such infrequent intervals that its value as an incentive is almost negligible. The average annual return per head amounted to less than £10 in the profit-sharing schemes in existence in 1924, and in times of depression it will obviously be less."[2]

The Will to Power. A motive that allows more scope to self-expression is the motive of personal ambition, of self-assertion, and of the exercise of mastery or power over others. This motive, rather than that of sheer cupidity, probably explains the energy and persistence and to some extent (along with favouring circumstance) the success, of the ' captains of industry.' To the majority of industrial workers the openings for such

[1] Miles. *op. cit.* p. 15.   [2] *Ibid.*, pp. 17–18.

display of mastery and organising ability are few and far between, and it is only perhaps a minority who are temperamentally 'master-ful' or 'push-ful,' and who in consequence would be inclined to seize such opportunities as might arise; but there is no doubt that hard work is done under the stimulus of this type of motive. Unfortunately the hard worker under such a stimulus is often a hard task-master in turn, and tends to be autocratic and regardless of the feelings and the needs of other men.

Other incentives. In the incentives so far examined the main appeal is based on the results and rewards of work rather than the interest of the work itself. And these results are considered in their relation to the producer rather than to the consumer, or to the community as a whole. The acquisitive conception of industry means " the denial that industry has any end or purpose other than the satisfaction of those engaged in it."[1] But work of some kinds has an intrinsic interest apart from the fact that it provides either a bare livelihood or a handsome profit to the worker; moreover, work of all kinds ministers, or should minister, to the needs of the community. The motives that are stimulated by the nature of the work itself and by the communal needs which work supplies may be called respectively the *creative* and the *social.*

Creative Motives.

(a) *Skill-hunger.* The most absorbing interest is to be found in work that satisfies what Dr. Jacks has described as 'skill-hunger,' the desire to use one's fingers and one's wits in the deft manipulation of material and in the creation of something beautiful or useful or both.

> " Man is a skill-hungry animal, hungry for skill in his body, hungry for skill in his mind, and never

Tawney. *The Acquisitive Society*, p. 43.

satisfied until that skill-hunger is appeased. . . .
The happiness that man's nature demands is impossible
until the creative part of him is awakened, until his
skill hunger is satisfied. . . . Till then, and till his
happiness begins to well up from within through this
self-active, creative life, man is living on a starvation
diet ; he is devitalised ; he is in a low condition ; he
is wanting in mind and body."[1]

How far this ' skill-hunger ' or ' instinct of workmanship ' (as Veblen calls it) can be satisfied under modern
methods of production we have already discussed.[2]
In the sense explained by Dr. Jacks it is nearer to play
and recreation than to work as it is ordinarily understood,
and we shall consider in dealing with the Leisure Problem[3]
the ways in which it may be satisfied by the expanding
leisure time that we may expect to find at man's disposal.
Meanwhile two considerations may be urged. One is
that it may be possible and desirable, while handing
over to machinery more and more of the work that is
found to be toilsome, wearisome or irksome, to reclaim
from machinery some forms of work that are peculiarly
apt to provide both joy to the worker and satisfaction to
the consumer. At any rate, we may expect to see an
increasing development of leisure arts and crafts that will
supply personal if not communal needs that mechanised
work and machine-made articles cannot so completely
satisfy.

The other consideration is that machine industry itself
is increasingly calling for creative skill not only in the
invention of new machines and processes, but also in
the design and execution of machine products in which
use and beauty are combined in new and satisfying
forms. The earlier designers of machine-made articles
tried to imitate as closely as possible the hand-made
article, instead of designing new forms both beautiful

---

[1] Jacks. *Education through Recreation*, pp. 39–49.
[2] Ch. V. *supra*.   [3] Ch. XIII *infra*.

and useful which were appropriate not only to the material in which the work was done, but to the purpose which it was intended to serve. To-day, architects, sculptors, and builders, as well as engineers and machine designers, are experimenting in new forms. But apart from the more novel and sometimes bizarre designs in building or in the construction of machines, there are widespread efforts to improve the standard of design in the everyday things of life,[1] which promise a fuller satisfaction both to producer and consumer.

(b) *Curiosity.*   This is the instinctive spring of learning and research which leads men to " ransack the ages " in the interests of historical knowledge, to explore the globe in the interests of geographical discovery and scientific information, and to experiment and speculate in the interests of every kind of scientific enquiry.   It has been directly or indirectly responsible for the technical advances of modern industry, and it prompts that disinterested interest which leads to progress both in scientific theory and in the application of science to the practical manipulation of nature.

(c) *Constructive Inventiveness.*   Closely bound up with the motive of curiosity is the motive which inspires the inventor.   An imaginative insight which is fertile in the ' eduction of correlates ' (to use Professor Spearman's term for a special kind of intellectual activity) is common to the creative artist and the constructive inventor.   Unfortunately scientific research and invention are not encouraged by manufacturers as they might be. We shall describe later instances of the waste of talent and suggestion that the experienced worker may be able to contribute.[2]

It is equally difficult for the scientific inventor (whether amateur or professional) to secure either a

---

[1] See the publications of the Design and Industries Association, and the *Report of the Gorell Committee on Industry and Art.*
[2] Chapter XI.

satisfactory trial of his discoveries or a fair amount for their patenting.   A craftsman and inventor of experience and ingenuity, Mr. W. S. Rogers, writes :

" The marketing of a patented invention in this country is difficult, partly because our manufacturers are conservative and ready to condemn a new device because it *is* new, or because it would disturb their routine of manufacture to embark on making it ; or in some cases because they hope to be able to secure the idea for themselves, without consideration, either by waiting until the inventor has abandoned his patent, or by shamelessly copying it with slight modification which they hope will disguise the fraud. I make these statements not as a disappointed inventor, for my temperament is such that I do not allow disappointments to worry me, but for the information of those who may be tempted to spend their time and money on ideas which they are sanguine enough to suppose will bring them an abundant money return.   After sufficient experience to test the matter I agree with the dictum of a brother mechanic with whom I discussed the question, that the only course open to the inventor, if he happen to have a good thing, and the means to do it, is to manufacture the article himself."

Mr. Rogers himself, being unable to manufacture, adopted the course of describing his inventions for the benefit of the readers of *Work*, to which journal he contributed some 220 articles in the course of five years.

Enterprising firms are increasingly adding a research and technical staff to their equipment or combining with other firms to employ a group of research workers, but the status and remuneration of qualified research workers are frequently inadequate to the importance of the function they perform.[1]

Before passing from the motives that arise from the

---

[1] Miles.   *The Problem of Incentives in Industry,* p. 53.

I

intrinsic interest of work, it is well to note that direct interest in the work itself is not always a completely satisfying motive. There are, it is true, artists and intellectual workers who can find a full and wide satisfaction in work which for them is indistinguishable from recreation. Edison is said to have worked for eighteen hours a day and to have made the statement, " My work is my recreation and my recreation is my work." But he is also said to have been " devoid of culture," and indifferent to history and art.[1] And if intellectual workers are liable to become narrowed and confined in outlook, craftsmen also tend to be so much absorbed in their work that they cannot look beyond it. There is a tell-tale passage in George Bourne's *The Wheelwright's Shop*, which suggests that in spite of his lyrical appreciation of the joy of craftsmanship, the interest of the work was often rather that of a close absorption and pre-occupation than a form of enjoyment. Speaking of a hard winter, he writes :—

" I have no recollection of feeling the cold at the time. The work was too interesting. The winter, the timber, the wheelwright's continuous tussle, the traditional adaptation, the skill and knowledge—all these factors, not thought of but felt, to the accompaniment of wood scents and saw-pit sounds, kept me from thinking of the cold—unless to appreciate that too. . . . It was no picnic. I was often tired to death at it. For I by no means conceived what a big thing I was taking so obscure a part in. In fact, more than once I tried to get clear of the business altogether, it was so fatiguing and it bored me so."

Set beside that passage this from Mr. Street's *Farmer's Glory* :—

" The old system of farming as described in the early part of this book was one which placed the farmer in a

<hr>

[1] Russell. *The Scientific Outlook*, p. 276.

yearly rut from which there was no escape. He did the same things, year after year, according to the season. Mistakes of one year were noted and avoided if possible in the next. You were kept so long busy and interested, that you had no time to think of much else, becoming narrow-minded possibly, but by experience a better performer each succeeding year."[1]

What these passages suggest is that certain forms of work—whether intellectual or practical—may be so absorbing that they claim too much of the mind of the worker. To be 'interested' literally means to be 'in it,' as R. L. Nettleship pointed out in an Essay on *Pleasure*, and he notes that the slang expression 'in it' and 'out of it' have retained something of this original meaning.[2] But just because being interested means being 'in it,' an absorbing interest means that you not only put a lot into it but that it takes a lot out of you. How much of you is engaged and how deeply in your work is an important matter. For if the interest be a narrow one it must have the effect of narrowing your outlook and your life, and the more so the longer the hours that the very interest of it compels you to devote to it. The work may fill your horizon, but is it desirable that one thing should so fill it ?

In view of these considerations there may be advantage in work that evokes more than one kind of interest, and especially in work that brings us into contact with other people.

Social Motives.

Since the function of industry is the provision of the human wants of the community, it might be expected that a sufficient motive to work would be found in the desire to serve the community. And indeed this motive is operative to a far greater extent than is often recognised.

[1] p. 291.
[2] *Philosophical Remains of R. L. Nettleship*, p. 17.

In the teaching and medical professions the service of obvious and often urgent human needs frequently takes precedence over all other claims ; and strength, leisure, and more lucrative forms of work are often sacrificed to the sense of vocation. It is this characteristic of the ' professions ' that leads Mr. Tawney to ask for a development of the professional spirit throughout the whole range of industrial work. A profession is a " body of men who carry on their work in accordance with rules designed to enforce certain standards both for the better protection of its members and for the better service of the public."[1] That professionalism may develop a narrow adherence to tradition and a tendency to sectionalism is not to be denied ;[2] it must at the same time be claimed that a standard of honour and devotion is expected of the doctor or the teacher far higher than is expected of the manufacturer or the industrial worker.

Yet why men should not put equal devotion into the making of houses or furniture or clothing, or the provision of food for the elementary needs of mankind, is difficult to understand ; the lines of professional and public service appeal to a sense of honour and justice which is already to be found in men's minds and which is to-day affronted by many things in industrial life that are unjust and ungenerous if not dishonourable, and consequently, even to those who practise them, frequently ' against the grain.'

But if service to the community is to be made an effective stimulus to work, certain conditions require to be fulfilled.

(1) To the ordinary man the ' community ' is a large and vague and distant abstraction, and can hardly be expected to be the object of devotion. You cannot love, as Dr. McTaggart once said, an indefinitely extended Post Office Directory. The ' community ' needs to be

---

[1] *The Acquisitive Society*, p. 106.
[2] cf. Wallas. *Our Social Heritage*, ch. vi.

translated into terms of readily imaginable men and women and children. For this purpose anything that brings the worker into immediate contact with the consumer of his work is an advantage. But this is rarely possible save in those forms of service which involve direct relations between producer and consumer. The professions of teaching, medicine, dentistry, and the law, as well as domestic, nursing and secretarial occupations, have here an advantage. The building trades, repair services and transport undertakings, rail or road, sea or air—are examples from industry. The distributive trades, especially in the shopping services, perhaps come next. But a vast number of industrial and commercial occupations provide no such opportunities of visible and tangible service. The work may be minutely subdivided, and the ultimate product may be distant or unascertainable, and the ultimate consumer may be at the farthest corner of the earth. But here the imagination of the worker might be helped if means were taken to secure and to circulate information as to the purpose of the work and its possible destination.

" Extreme specialisation of work has hitherto tended to produce an employee who knows nothing of what goes on save in the small sphere of labour in which he is engaged. Clearly, the remedy lies in giving the novice some knowledge of the history and aims of the concern, and of the previous and subsequent operations undergone by the material on which he works, from its raw state to the finished product—in instructing him, in short, in all matters which will encourage interest and loyalty to the concern, and will help him to realise the particular social service to the community which he is performing."[1]

We have already seen the importance of interest in the

[1] Myers. *Business Rationalisation*, p. 46.

outcome of a man's work in providing him with a sense of satisfaction in the doing of it.[1]

A Branch Manageress in an ironmongery shop, who was responsible for training new and young assistants, writes :—

> " I tried to make them take a real and intelligent interest in the commodities and the meaning of those which they sold (*e.g.*, Nettlefold's screws give one a good lead in describing and discussing movements and developments in the steel industry). I arranged talks on these things also. This enabled me to feel that buying and selling was not entirely a vulgar business of pushing large quantities of goods on an unwilling public in order to justify the receiving of a wage."

(2) It may be difficult to bring home the significance and value of a job if the ultimate consumer is remote and uncertain, but its more immediate service to the welfare of the undertaking in which a worker is employed and of all his fellow workers in it is a secondary object of no mean importance. Here the incentives of emulation and appreciation are not often fostered as they might be. One of the most interesting features of the new factory discipline in Russia is the use that is made of these incentives in promoting the furtherance of the Five Year Plan.

> " Here and there an inscription on the wall newspaper sharply criticised or glowingly praised particular workers. Or, in some factories, a judgment upon weak personal links in the factory machine was passed by the sending of delinquents to draw their pay at a pay-office shaped like an enormous vodka-bottle. My mind recalled Robert Owen's ' silent monitors,' the coloured cubes suspended over the working-place of each employee at the New Lanark mill and showing by the

---

[1] *Supra* p. 107.

coloured face, blue, black, yellow or white, the standard of conduct attained. . . . In our industrial revolution, the new factory discipline was often felt to be a painful thing. The tyranny of the factory bell ('clocking-on' in our own day), the 'bate-book' or system of fines here a century ago, the stern driving of the overseer or foreman —these are replaced in the Russian factory of to-day by an urgent collective opinion. 'We look to you, Director', I read on an inscription outside the general manager's office of a Moscow cotton mill, 'to see to it that we fulfil all our quota under the plan and more.' Think of the joy it would give an L.M.S. porter to pin such a notice outside Sir Josiah Stamp's office at Euston. A belated industrial revolution. . . . . Yes, and the workers' own." [1]

The Five Year Plan suggests the value as an incentive of aiming at a certain standard of work to be attained in a given period.

" The setting of some definite standard, especially if voluntarily determined by the workers themselves, gives a target at which to aim : some department of a store, for example, may set out to attain a definite turnover at the annual sale."[2]

One of the drawbacks of the large-scale organisation of business to-day is in the loss of personal contact and appreciation.

" One of the bitterest comments that could ever be uttered against one of our large present-day organisations was made by an old employee of a firm. 'We don't count nowadays,' he said, and he then described how his old boss used to praise and also to criticise his work. In the drive of modern industrial life many departmental managers and foremen have entirely lost

---

[1] H. L. Beales, in an article on *Industrial Development in Russia*, in the *Highway*, Dec., 1932.
[2] Miles. *The Problem of Incentives in Industry*, p. 23.

sight of the important incentive of personal appreciation and encouragement."[1]

A Post Office sorter writes of some foremen or supervisors :—

" They are solicitous only for the work.   I do not exist.   I get no thought at all unless I am absent ; then I am conspicuous. . . .   This fatiguing hopelessness grows into an obsession out of which many workers never emerge.   Their minds are smudged with a sort of factory drabness."

Group loyalty is a powerful motive of which far more could be made.   But the groups which are concerned in industry to-day are frequently opposed in aim and interest, and the loyalty of a worker to his mates will often conflict, and not coincide, with loyalty to the organisation as a whole.   One of the attractions of the Guild Socialist idea and of some of the experiments that attempted to embody it was its emphasis on industry as a self-governing service in which the whole personnel of the industry—management, technicians, and operatives—were to combine their interest, good-will and responsibility in the service of the industry, and through it of the community.

(3) But if the motive of professional service is to be stimulated more fully in industry, it must still be recognised that along with a readiness to serve the community there is also a pardonable and indeed legitimate solicitude for self and family.   Consequently, we are likely to secure the interest and co-operation of each of the groups of participants in industry—managers, technicians, clerical staff and operatives—only if we are able to guarantee some measure of security to each, and in addition some degree of control over the conditions of their work.   Here again, one of the attractive novelties of the Guild idea is the system of payment by which the

[1] *op. cit.* p. 22.

wage-earner is put on much the same footing as the salary-earner of to-day, and the labour contract becomes (like the marriage contract) one which is entered on for better for worse, in sickness or in health, in bad weather or in fine, in employment or in unemployment. Thus the primary and urgent need of security is met, but the motive to it is united, not with the motive of gain, but with the motive of social service.

The future lies with a community that shall contrive to avail itself of the skill and interest, the public service and professional honour of its members in the organisation and development of its industries. For in the creative interest of doing a piece of work well and soundly and the public-spirited desire to do it for the benefit of the community we have the highest and most effective motives that can be enlisted in the sphere of industry.

CHAPTER XI

SCIENTIFIC MANAGEMENT AND LABOUR

WE have already seen[1] that the application of scientific
method to the technical conditions of work has aimed at
substituting exact knowledge and accurate performance
for traditional hearsay and rough-and-ready rule of thumb.

But while industrialists have been quick to take
advantage of scientific research in the invention of
machinery and the development of technical processes,
they have been less ready to apply scientific method to
the organisation of work and the management of industry.
To-day, indeed, we hear on all sides of the importance of
' Planning ' in both economic and political affairs, and
' Rationalisation ' is the slogan of the hour.   As yet, however, it is a ' blessed word ' rather than a widely accepted
and practical policy; and the world of industry and
commerce still presents the picture of a planless and
unsystematic muddle.

If we are to make a distinction between Scientific
Management and Rationalisation we may use the former
term for the application of scientific methods of organisation to the individual business unit and the latter for their
application to a number of related concerns or to the
problems of a whole industry.[2]

Scientific Management, or ' Taylorism ' as it was at one
time called (after the name of F. W. Taylor, who carried
out pioneer experiments in the United States), dates from
about 1882.   Its main aim was " to apply psychology so
as to get the maximum quantity of production from the

---

[1] Chapter V, *supra.*
[2] Myers. *Business Rationalisation*, p. 20.

minimum expenditure of human energy." The Taylor system meant, among other things, the careful assessment of the time and energy required for a particular job, the methodical instruction of the worker so that he should perform the job within the allotted time and with a minimum expenditure of energy, and the calculation of the piece-rate pay " at such a figure as would penalise the man who did not put forth normal effort, but reward *well* those who exceeded it."[1]

From Taylor's first experiments in 'Efficiency Engineering' the movement has made enormous strides, especially in America. Taylor and Gantt worked out a system of scientific management for the Bethlehem Steel Works at the beginning of this century, and other systems followed in rapid succession. This is not the place to describe the progress of the movement in detail.

I propose to select for discussion those aspects of it that most nearly affect for good or ill the workers whose output and efficiency Scientific Management has been concerned to improve.

Here, as in our consideration of machinery, we find the gains and losses difficult to disentangle and assess. That ' efficiency methods ' have eliminated physical fatigue and to that extent improved the worker's lot is undeniable ; that they have often been applied in such a way as to subject him to a greater nervous strain is also undeniable. Let us first see how the application of what is known as Motion Study is calculated to eliminate fatigue.

A skilled performance, as we have said above,[2] will be marked by the elimination of superfluous and inefficient movements and the selection of those which are best suited to the purpose. The result is seen in an ease and grace of movement which is admired by all observers. It is often the worker or player who appears to be putting forth least effort who is in fact most effective.

---

[1] Watts. *Psychological Problems of Industry*, p. 105.
[2] Chapter V.

" It generally comes as a surprise to an outsider to find, as is so often the case, that the workers who appear to be lazy are in reality doing far more than the apparently energetic."[1]

This is illustrated in the older crafts where men have learnt by tradition and experience to conserve their energy and to apply it with a minimum of waste.

" Many people think that the agricultural labourer of those days was slow in his movements. This is incorrect. He looked slow, I grant you, but the experience of countless ages had discovered the simplest and easiest way of doing his manifold laborious tasks, and years of practice had transformed his gnarled and clumsy hands into extraordinarily deft and dexterous instruments. Also, he struck a gait at any job which he could keep up from daylight to dark, day after day. Any attempt to hurry him was disastrous. He considered it to be a slight upon him, and that you didn't realise that he always gave of his best."[2]

But mere practice and familiarity is not a guarantee of efficiency, and habit may as easily confirm a series of mistaken movements as a series of effective ones. These, like all habitual actions, it is difficult to unlearn. Hence the importance of training the worker, and especially the novice, in the most easy and efficient movements for the performance of any operation.

A pioneer investigator in the field of what has come to be called ' motion study ' was Mr. F. B. Gilbreth, an American ' engineer,' who applied it to the work of bricklaying. He devised various means of eliminating unnecessary movements. Whereas the ordinary bricklayer had been accustomed to lower and raise " continually through a space of two feet or so a hundredweight and a half of ' bricklayer,' not to speak of tools and materials, every time he needed a brick or a trowel of mortar,"

---

[1] Welch and Miles. *op. cit.*, p. 70.
[2] Street. *Farmer's Glory*, p. 42.

Gilbreth's bricklayer worked on an adjustable scaffold providing for a constant adjustment of loose bricks, mortar-box, and ' bricklayer ' in relation to the rising wall. In place of a performance requiring 18 separate movements (some extremely fatiguing) he devised an easier and more efficient one of 5 movements. Numerous other improvements were suggested for application not only to bricklaying but to other occupations. In particular, Gilbreth insisted on the provision of work-tables, chairs and tools adapted to the worker, and carried his enquiry into the conditions of lighting, etc., of the work place.

Gilbreth's work has been followed up by later investigators, not only in America, but more recently by the British National Institute of Industrial Psychology which has carried out investigations in several different industries. In a chocolate factory they recommended a new arrangement of the packing bench ; rhythmical arm movements in place of irregular ones ; and other improvements which raised the output by 35 to 40 per cent. and earned the gratitude of the employees because they ' went home less tired.' In a colliery, study was made of the character and rhythm of the miner's movements, the best shape and size of his tools, and the intensity and diffusion of the light of his lamp. " The results were increases of output of from 10 to 14 per cent. through an improved type of light, and 16 per cent. through other studies, while at the same time the quality of the coal (as regards the inclusion of dirt) was improved." " These investigations were heartily welcomed by the miners, who repeatedly expressed their approval of the improved conditions of work, pointing out other subjects of investigation that were likely to result both in increased comfort and increased output."[1] Similar results have followed the Institute's investigations in a number of widely different industries.

[1] See *Reports of National Institute of Industrial Psychology.*

In the course of such investigations use is made of the instrument first devised by Gilbreth—the ' chrono-cyclegraph.' A small electric light is attached to the wrist of the worker and his movements are photographed by means of a special camera, which indicate the time of the process by a series of dashes. Cinematograph photos can also be taken for reproduction by ' slow motion ' on a screen. Again, photographs seen through stereoscopic lenses, show the movements as a series of lines, which can be copied in the form of a wire model, and this can be used for the instruction of the workers. In such photographs the more efficient movements come out in single lines and graceful curves : while " inefficiency is shewn by blurs and tangles and uncertainties."[1] Again the photographs reveal striking differences (as between efficient and inefficient workers) in the number of motions required. While the best worker in a margarine factory was able to wrap a pat of margarine in 4 distinct motions, another girl took over 24 motions in the same process.

But while the most efficient movements and the most graceful rhythm in the abstract can be arrived at in this way, it must be remembered that there are great indi-vidual differences between workers in respect of the method and rhythm that are either ' natural ' to them or to which they have become accustomed, and it would be a mistake to suppose (as Taylor and Gilbreth did), that there is one ideal method which can be represented by a *standard* speed and a *standard* motion.

This is now realised by workers in the field of Industrial Psychology.

" Mainly through the increasing influence of. . . . the industrial psychologist, it has become recognised that there is no " one best way ' of carrying out work,

---

[1] Watts. *op. cit.* For further illustrations see Welch and Miles, *Industrial Psychology in Practice.*

that different styles are suited to different workers, and that the principles of training should be based rather on the prevention of the worker from acquiring undoubtedly bad habits of work, than on forcing him to adopt a uniform method which may be unsuited to him."[1]

If movement study were to lead to a mechanisation of the work and a standardisation of the worker, the last state might be worse than the first, nor would efficiency itself be promoted by methods that so flagrantly ignored the human factor.

This indeed was the charge that was made, and not without justification, against the earlier experiments in Scientific Management. In 1913 an enquiry was conducted in America, under the chairmanship of Professor Hoxie, into the results of Scientific Management as they affected labour.

The Hoxie Report contains the conclusions of this enquiry[2] and the following were the principal labour objections to Scientific Management as conducted up to that time.

(1) That the lion's share of the increased profits resulting from Scientific Management goes to capital, however much wages may be advanced.

(2) That the various forms of ' premium bonus ' and other systems of piece-rate payment are not fairly operated, but are accompanied by ' rate-cutting ' dodges.

(3) That workers become unemployed as a consequence of the adoption of labour-saving devices both in machinery and arrangement of work.

(4) That the system involves ' speeding-up ' and ' driving ' and subjects the workers to nervous strain.

---

[1] Myers. *Business Rationalisation*, p. 38.
[2] See Hoxie. *Scientific Management and Labour.*

(5) That the subdivision and standardisation of processes lessens the individuality of the worker, destroys his craft skill, makes for monotony, and turns him into a mechanical automaton.

(6) That the system interferes with collective bargaining and weakens the hold of Trade Unions.

(7) That the system involves autocratic control by 'functional bosses' and lessens the interest and responsibility of the worker.

It cannot be said that these objections have been to any considerable extent removed since the Hoxie enquiry took place, although many firms in this country have introduced and operated the methods of Scientific Management with more regard for the susceptibilities of the workers and with more success in securing their co-operation than the earlier American pioneers. The objections, however, apply rather to the methods by which Scientific Management has been carried out than to Scientific Management itself, and even where they can be sustained against the methods, they do not invalidate the principle. If the application of psychology to industry has been accompanied by practices that are open to objection, that is no more an argument against applied psychology than the perversion of chemistry in poison-gas research is an argument against applied chemistry. It is significant that Lenin said in 1918, " We must introduce in Russia the study and the teaching of the Taylor system and its systematic trial and adaptation."

Some of the objections outlined above apply to all forms of mechanisation and mass-production and we have already discussed the problems arising from the subdivision of processes, ' speeding-up ' and monotony. We shall deal later with the problem of ' technological unemployment.'[1]   Here let us examine the objection that Scientific Management involves methods of autocratic control which lessen the responsibility of the worker and

[1] See Chapter XII.

weaken the power of his collective organisations. The Taylor method was particularly vulnerable at this point. It involved a system of industrial direction and supervision that imposed a rigid regimentation of the workers, under which they had to obey without thought or question the instructions given from above. Taylor himself was explicit on this point :—

> " All possible brain-work should be removed from the shop and centred in the planning department, leaving for the foremen and gang-bosses work strictly executive in its nature. . . . Each man must . . . grow accustomed to receiving and obeying instructions, covering details, large and small, which in the past have been left to his judgment."[1]

But the Taylor system, while autocratic in character, followed a plan of ' functional management ' rather than that of a hierarchy of superior officials and subordinates of the ' military ' type. Departments and officials were to be differentiated in accordance with specific functions in place of the general supervision by ' general ' manager and single ' foreman.' For example, in the Planning Department, the ' instruction card ' man drew up instructions for the jobs, specifying tools required, speed, time, etc., the ' route ' man planned the traffic through the shops, the ' time and cost ' man recorded the time and adjusted the pay, and the ' disciplinarian ' dealt with order and disputes. Again, in the Performing Department the ' gang-bosses ' gave direct instructions, the ' speed-boss ' supervised the rate of machines, the ' repair boss ' overhauled machines, and the ' inspector ' supervised the quality of the work. These are examples which indicate a part only of an elaborate system of ' functional management,' involving an unwieldy multiplication of unproductive workers.[2] That the system outlined is

---

[1] Cited by Watts. *op. cit.*, p. 104.

[2] On " over-functionalisation," see Myers. *Business Rationalisation,* ch. ii.

K

over-complicated and elaborate does not invalidate the need for differentiation of the various managerial and technical functions in large-scale industry, and while more recent theories of management aim at simpler and more economical methods they owe not a little to the 'functional' idea.   In particular, benefits have resulted from a better co-ordination of departments by allotting to special officers the responsibility for planning and routeing the flow of orders, material and work, estimating costs, selecting and training personnel, organising transport, and supervising marketing and distribution.

The worker is not concerned to complain of any of the developments in industrial organisation that mean a higher standard of managerial and technical efficiency in these directions.   What he has reason to resent is the failure to provide the means by which he may exercise an intelligent interest in the more efficient administration of the concern in which he is employed, and a share of responsibility over matters in which he is particularly concerned or in which he feels he has a contribution to offer from his own experience and knowledge.

Among such matters the arrangement and improvement of his actual job and the conditions accompanying its performance, the engagement, promotion or dismissal of his immediate fellow workers, and the prospects of the concern as they affect his standard of life and his future employment, are those which most nearly concern him. To provide opportunities by which he may be both informed and consulted about such matters is to go a long way toward giving him the sense that he is a responsible partner in the enterprise and not merely an interchangeable part of its machinery.

The fact that the vast majority of workers have no voice in the control of the concern in which they are engaged means that they acquire an exaggerated sense of inferiority which shews itself either in the listless acquiescence of the Robot or in the unrest and agitation of the Rebel.

A strike is often welcomed not so much for the ostensible aim which it is designed to effect—the protection of a wage-standard or the resistance to an act of victimisation—as because it opens the floodgates to a mass of incoherent and inarticulate unrest and protest and gives for a time to those who thus assert themselves a sense that they possess after all a power and an importance in the scheme of things.

Mr. R. M. Fox writes :—

" No one who has been, as I have been, in a workshop where that sense of exaltation, solidarity, power and expectancy called strike-feeling has swept through the works can doubt that it is partly a psychological reaction against mechanical routine."

And he adds a significant observation :—

" If this flood of generous aspirations is ever harnessed to practical ends in the same way as the power of the workshop is used to drive the machines, there is no social reconstruction too big for it to bring about."[1]

Of all the forms of ' waste ' in industry which it should be the business of scientific organisation to eliminate, the one which has received least attention is the waste of the intelligence, the experience, and the good-will which the workers themselves might contribute, but which hitherto has been thoughtlessly ignored or deliberately slighted.

Here and there schemes for the collection and reward of suggestions or inventions devised by workers are adopted ; here and there schemes for the consultation of workers through their representation on Shop Committees, Works Councils, or Trade Union organisations are in operation ; but such machinery is not only rarely

[1] *The Triumphant Machine*, pp. 57–58.

found but rarely treated as a matter of the first importance.

Those of my informants who have had acquaintance with such schemes express themselves as frankly disappointed with their half-hearted and ineffective application.

An electrician writes :—

" There was once a Joint Committee set up as a result of negotiations between the Trade Union and the employers. The young and foolish said, ' Ah, at last, workers' control ! ' The old ones said, ' Not bloody likely,' and they were right. For we were told that a box was to be placed for our suggestions (' Oh, oh,' says the gang, ' now for it——'). But we further learned that such questions as hours, wages, conditions, etc., were outside our jurisdiction—it appeared as though the only thing we had any voice in at all was the Annual Trip to Blackpool ! So the only suggestion ever placed in the box was couched in most unparliamentary language and told the Management what to do with its Works Council. (They must have taken this advice, for it was never heard of again.)"

Others describe more ambitious and promising experiments, and they do not always blame the Management for their failure. A railwayman who has served on a Departmental Committee says : " Unfortunately, the men do not as a rule use these committees to the full." Printers describe the arrangements by which the ' Father of the Chapel ' or Shop Steward, with his Committee, exercises " a big voice in control and arbitration." But one of them adds that " alterations of working and additions of plant are matters on which the men would not be consulted unless some violation of a trade union regulation is involved."

A Post Office worker with some experience of a Whitley Committee writes :—

" My own experience is that such committees are

not particularly successful. A live trade union branch and a broad-minded and efficient local chief are much more likely to achieve practical progress. Indeed, in practice, given these conditions, there is a happy liaison which makes for *influence* by the workers if not actual control. These conditions are, however, not frequently found."

One often gets the impression that the primary need is not so much that of a particular type of machinery of consultation (important as some form of machinery may be) as of an atmosphere of confidence and co-operation. This is the more difficult to secure in a large-scale impersonal undertaking, and it is on that account a question of increasing importance in view of the expanding scale of business organisation. It is rare to find the kind of atmosphere described by a steel-worker in the following :

" The works I was employed at, though part of a large concern, had a tradition of friendly relations between men and employers or their representatives. The general manager had graduated from the smelting furnaces as also had his brother, the works manager. They knew each individual as ' Tom,' ' Harry ' or ' Dai.' The usual method by which grievances were ventilated or wrongs adjusted was that of negotiation between the works representative of the trade union branch and the manager. I served as works representative for some years and found the manager, although a keen business man, invariably fair in his dealings. We had no measure of control as far as management or policy of the firm was concerned, but any changes which became, in the opinion of the firm, necessary, were discussed with the representatives of the men. For instance, new machines were to be put into operation in the gas-producing plant, which meant that instead of six men only three would be required. We were invited to discuss the method of arranging the men so as to mitigate as far as possible the effects of installing the new machines.   Then the firm invited us to discuss the best way of meeting the prevailing trade depression."

Two points emerge from a consideration of testimonies like those I have cited, and which I could supplement from numerous conversations on the question.   One is that the foundations of a better system of co-operation and self-government in industry must be laid in the local unit of production and even in the workshop itself. No grandiose superstructure of Industrial Councils will be stable unless it is based upon the sound working co-operation of the staff and personnel of the individual department and workshop.   The other is that the avoidance of friction and harmonious settlement of grievances and disputes are more likely to occur where there is a genuine attempt to secure co-operation in the day-to-day working of a concern and prior to, rather than after, any contemplated changes.   It is the habit of consultation that is important, and if that has not been acquired, it is not likely that sporadic efforts to procure agreements after trouble has arisen will be assured of success.

This is an additional reason for attaching importance to the enlistment of the worker's interest in the technical improvement and general advancement of the industry in which he is employed.   If he is discouraged from contributing his experience and intelligence he can hardly be expected to contribute his good-will.   Yet it is rare that any genuine attempt is made to draw upon this fund of experience and insight.

And it is still more rare that any just recognition is given to contributions that the worker does provide. As a consequence of this utter lack of recognition or reward, the worker ceases to interest himself in the efficient performance or arrangement of his work, and his consequent apathy if not antipathy turns a potential asset into an actual liability. Again and again I have received reports which have drawn attention to the futility of efforts to suggest improvements. A miner writes :—

" I made several suggestions for the use of methods which would lighten, improve and cut down the costs of certain jobs, but because these methods involved work being done by other departments, they were turned down, even when it was easy to prove that my methods were far more economical. Several of these suggestions have been adopted since I left owing to increased work for a decreased staff."

Another miner says :—

" We are not consulted in any way. However much we might know that certain practices are inefficient, dangerous, or tyrannous, any suggestions, even for efficiency, are resented by ' bosses,' or treated spitefully. This is very irritating indeed, and creates and emphasises frustration. In recent times, even despair and acquiescence in these conditions have been engendered."

A worker employed by a public utility company writes :—

" At present, those engaged in industry are not encouraged to take interest in its management. I forwarded criticisms and suggestions concerning my own firm. . . . The Secretary of the Committee to whom I sent these suggestions suavely informed me that my letter was the result of wide reading and deep thinking, and, in a sense, the contents were true, but asked me if I were prepared to endure the wrath of officials who were in a position to give vent to their wrath. My manager then interviewed me, tincturing flattery with a not too subtle warning, that my interests should not wander from the sphere in which I was immediately engaged. After mature consideration I came to the conclusion that I valued security more than self-respect, and therefore withdrew my letter."

Another informant tells me of a Post Office mechanic who invented a new and much improved type of instrument.

" It is a rule of the Post Office that anything invented by a member of the staff must be handed to the Department. Every three months or so Headquarters issue a list of awards in return for suggested improvements in existing apparatus and for inventions. The amounts usually vary between £1 and £4. £5 to £10 are exceptional awards."

The mechanic in this case was offered no more than the customary award, and knowing the value of his invention he resigned his position. After interviewing the Company that held the original patents to manufacture the instruments, he received a good cheque for his patent rights and a highly salaried situation on their Research staff.

" The most ironical part of the whole affair is that for each of these new instruments the Post Office instal they have to pay their erstwhile mechanic a substantial royalty."

Why was he not transferred to the Research Department of the Post Office ? It would appear that invention is still discouraged by the Barnacles of the Circumlocution Offices of State.

An engineer who has had many years' experience in investigating costs of production both in Government and private undertakings, has recently urged the wider recognition of the worker as a thinking being, and recommends in particular more adequate encouragement of suggestions, the dissemination of information about costs and the higher ' politics ' of the firm, and means by which the workers' representatives can co-operate in rate-setting. On suggestion schemes he writes :—

" I have seen quite a number of such schemes in operation, but most of them have become dormant after a time, not necessarily because ideas were stagnant, but because of the impression that by far the major portion of any saving effected went, not to the suggestor, but to the firm. It ought not to be beyond the scope of any concern to devise means for keeping such schemes alive, to the mutual advantage of worker and employer. A statement showing the savings effected as the result of a suggestion, with a percentage payment to the author over an agreed number of years, would probably solve the problem."[1]

At present only too often suggestions may be rewarded not with a remuneration but a snub. A carter engaged in the delivery of coal writes : " Whenever I re-arranged the work in any way I am convinced it was beneficial to both myself and employer," but he adds, " Servility is better liked than efficiency."

Nothing is more galling to the worker than to be compelled to go on doing things in a way he knows to be wrong, or at least wasteful and inefficient, because he knows that if he speaks about the matter he will be told, " You are not here to think, you are here to obey orders." One who has heard such a reply given again and again remarks that it is small wonder that daily work comes to be regarded as " bread-winning and nothing else."[2]

We come back, then, to the same point that was emphasised in discussing responsibility as a motive to work,[3] namely, that unless men feel that they are engaged in an undertaking which calls for a high standard of

---

[1] T. H. Hargrave, in *The Worker's Point of View*, p. 148.
[2] From an article entitled *What Factory Work Feels Like* (*The Friend*, Sept. 23rd, 1932).
[3] *Supra*, p. 115.

service and invites them to give of their best their work is likely to be listless and inefficient. If Scientific Management is to be successfully applied to industry, it must evoke the fullest measure of co-operation from the whole personnel.

If not, if the human factor is neglected, if the workers' experience and interest and powers of responsible collaboration are wasted, ' efficiency ' methods will be inefficient, ' scientific ' management will be unscientific, and ' rationalisation ' will be irrational.

CHAPTER XII

RATIONALISATION AND UNEMPLOYMENT

THE movement known as ' rationalisation ' represents the culmination of a number of allied tendencies which have been taking place over the whole field of industry for some time past but which have been accelerated since the War. Among these tendencies are the growth of various forms of industrial combination in place of disordered competition, the growth of mechanisation, and the growth of Scientific Management and efficiency methods. Rationalisation means the deliberate and systematic encouragement of these tendencies with a view to the most economical and efficient organisation of production and distribution. The term *Rationalisierung* was first employed in Germany to describe a narrower and more specific aim dictated by the circumstances of the post-war industrial situation, especially in the Ruhr. This was the aim of ' rationing ' the output of certain industrial establishments " to keep it within the limits of current market demands,"[1] and of effecting simultaneously a reduction in costs. But the term has come to be used for a far more comprehensive policy that is being taken up by industrialists the world over. At the World Economic Conference held at Geneva in 1927 rationalisation was defined as covering

> " The methods of technique and organisation designed to secure the minimum waste of either effort or material. It includes the scientific organisation of labour, standardisation both of material and products, simplification of processes, and improvements in the system of transport and marketing."

[1] Meakin. *The New Industrial Revolution*, p. 17.

The late Lord Melchett claimed for it a four-fold advantage—that it allows of scientific allocation of capital expenditure and the financing of new plant and up-to-date equipment, that it encourages specialisation, the closing of inefficient concerns, and the concentration of management and of commercial propaganda, selling and other expenses; that it prevents waste and overlapping— e.g., duplication of stocks, unnecessary varieties in size and form of commodities, or overlapping of research; that it provides insurance against fluctuations of markets and prices and by promoting an orderly system of purchasing raw materials and marketing commodities facilitates a world review of economic needs and supplies.

" The rationalisation of industry, then, is an attempt to adjust the means of production to the probable means of consumption, and so to regulate prices that, instead of curves rising and falling like the contours of the Alps, there should be a fairly level roadway of prices along which trade and commerce could move."[1]

It is clear that while Scientific Management can be applied to a quite small undertaking, the further aims of rationalisation require large-scale organisation and the linking up of undertakings within an industry, or as between allied industries, and that ultimately international groupings are necessary to secure complete co-ordination. The scale and form of organisation will differ from industry to industry, and any study of industrial combination reveals a great variety of different structures already in existence. Simple amalgamations, trusts and ' mergers,' horizontal or vertical combines or cartels, pooling and price-fixing and selling arrangements —innumerable forms of combination are to be found. We are not concerned here with their description, but certain points may be noted about their effects.

(a) The enlargement of the business unit, while to a

[1] Mond. *Industry and Politics*, p. 211.

large extent eliminating competition within a given area, may have the effect of intensifying competition on an international scale. The oil industry is a familiar example.[1]

(b) Efficiency has not always followed from large combinations, owing to over-capitalisation and lack of directive ability to control an unwieldy concern. Dr. Myers has made effective use of biological analogies to show the absurdity of supposing that huge business organisations are likely to be always the most suitable or that they should supplant the smaller concerns entirely.[2]

(c) The monopoly powers of combines and ' rings ' have led to restriction of output and artificial raising of prices. This policy reaches its *reductio ad absurdum* in the burning of wheat and coffee or the destruction of rubber.

(d) The increasing power of combines—both national and international—calls for some form of State supervision and ultimately of international control in the interests alike of the worker and the consumer.

We shall return later to some of these points. In the meantime let us look at some examples of mechanisation following from rationalisation policy, for although rationalisation does not of necessity involve any mechanical changes it is that aspect which primarily concerns us here.

The process in Germany began in the Ruhr coalfields with an endeavour by concerted action to bring about the lowest possible production costs while maintaining effective regulation of output. This meant first a series of amalgamations and re-groupings which made possible the closing down of unproductive or obsolete plants. Next, it meant the modernisation of equipment, and the introduction of the most up-to-date methods of mechanisation—in coal-cutting, where the seams were

---

[1] The oil companies have now formed an international cartel, involving restriction of exports by quotas.

[2] *Business Rationalisation*, p. 8.

suitable, in haulage, for the conveyance of the men and of the coal, in loading and unloading the cages, and in screening and washing. Next it meant the development of the ' coal-using ' as distinct from the ' coal-getting ' side of the industry, by means of coking, by-product, and power enterprises all in turn reconstructed on the most up-to-date lines. Long distance mains for the supply of gas and electricity to municipalities and industrial undertakings were established, with remarkable results in the form of low prices to the consumers.

Turning to steel, the great Stinnes ' vertical trust ' comprising all stages of manufacture and transport from the raw material to the finished article by means of a colossal conglomeration of coal, iron, steel, engineering, shipping and other trades, gave place for a time to a series of ' horizontal ' combinations—i.e., the merging of works turning out similar products—with arrangements for regulating output and prices. Then in pursuit of rationalisation policy came the building up of a gigantic Trust controlling 100 blast furnaces, 150 furnaces in steel works, and 48 collieries, which proceeded to carry out a scheme of rationalisation by cutting out overlapping departments and inefficient equipment, concentrating in particular works on specialised production, standardising the products, such as rails, bars, plates, etc., and effecting further economies by bulk purchase of materials, pooling of scientific and technical research, and centralising the marketing of products. While preserving central control over general policy, a large measure of autonomy was allowed in the management of the groups of specialised undertakings. Arrangements with the Iron and Steel firms of France, Belgium and Luxembourg, and later with those of Austria, Hungary and Czechoslovakia, have brought about something like a European Combine, from which, partly from policy and partly from lack of internal consolidation, the British Steel Industry has stood apart.

Here I am chiefly concerned with the extent to which these large-scale combinations have facilitated the process of mechanisation, and the best example of this is to be found in the great German electrical power undertaking.

" Germany is now covered by a network of high voltage overland transmission lines and secondary cables carrying the current from the transforming stations to the users.   The organisation is on a zone basis, corresponding roughly, but not completely, to the territories of the federated States."[1]

In each zone the control of administration is vested in a sort of public corporation either directly or indirectly responsible to the State or municipal authorities and with a limited interest on the capital invested.   The distribution is in the hands of municipal and other public authorities.

Mr. Meakin gives a remarkable account of the way in which brown coal is mechanically ' quarried ' for the purpose of fuel for a number of the power stations.

" Here one sees attained the utmost limits of mechanisation.   In the main the lignite is mined from wide open quarries, and gigantic electrical scooping machines are used for removing the ' overlay ' of earth and for taking up the lignite, which resembles fairly dry peat in texture.   The waggons conveying the fuel from the quarry to the station are emptied automatically into enormous hoppers, from which it passes on conveying belts to the hoppers over the furnaces.   One man, sitting at a switchboard and receiving communications from the power house engineers indicating their steam requirements, controls the flow of the lignite into eighty furnaces.   In the great boiler houses the personnel consists of a few mechanics.   The ashes fall from the furnace bars into a funnel where they are sprayed by water and drawn

[1] Meakin. *The New Industrial Revolution*, p. 145.

by compressed air suction through pipes back to the cleared spaces of the quarry. From start to finish no manual labour, in the ordinary accepted sense of the word, is employed in the process of winning from ten to fifteen thousand tons of brown coal per day. . . . In this organisation for the large-scale concentrated generation of electricity, . . . we see the application of the chief principles of rationalisation—central control of production, the most complete mechanisation attainable to eliminate the heaviest and lowest-paid forms of labour, and the avoidance of waste both of human effort and material resources—under a system of socialised ownership, combined with a modified form of ordinary industrial and commercial administration."[1]

In France as well as in Germany—though to a less thorough extent—rationalisation measures have been taken since the war, and not only in mining, metallurgy and engineering, shipping and transport, but also in chemicals, dyestuffs, drugs, artificial silks, textile dyeing, and in the rubber, sugar, potash, paper and cinema trades. In particular, it may be noted that the devastation of the industrial areas of France and Belgium made possible a complete re-equipment and modern mechanisation of the coal and steel industries.

Lord Melchett quotes a Commercial Councillor in Paris who says :

" This larger scale, standardised and factory specialised production by organisations both with numerous owned and numerous affiliated factories in various parts of France, has made notable progress ; and great French firms have increased to a marked extent their own international activities both as regards producing and marketing. One conspicuous result of these transformations is the definite entry of France

---

[1] Meakin. *op. cit.*, pp. 148–150.

into the lists as a considerable competitor in the world markets for goods of current consumption."[1]

In this country, apart from the great Mond combine—Imperial Chemical Industries, the policy of rationalisation has not so far been adopted save in a piecemeal and tentative fashion. English combines have been most successful hitherto where the economic unit has remained relatively small (e.g. in tobacco, wall-paper, whisky, and cement concerns). The Lever soap trust[2] and the Coats cotton merger represent the type of large combine with which we have been most familiar. In the heavy industries we have made very little headway. The mining industry is a conspicuous example of our slowness to adopt rationalisation measures—in spite of the recommendations of several Commissions of Enquiry. While the Rhenish Westphalian Coal Syndicate controls about seventy per cent. of the total output of coal in Germany and the greater part of her export trade, in Great Britain we had until recently about 613 colliery companies and about 3,000 mines, and the mines that have been closed down have been closed down not in pursuit of a rational plan but according to the hazards of circumstance. The process of securing amalgamations and setting up co-operative selling agencies has been carried further of late, but the pace is slow and follows no systematic plan.[3]

Obsolete methods of production are still to be found even in pits that are capable of being brought under the new technical methods. It would appear that only a national policy of re-organisation—either by nationalisation or by the development of large groupings—can provide the capital required to scrap the obsolete plants and to reorganise the technique of production as well as the methods of coal-using and coal-marketing. The

---

[1] *Industry and Politics, p.* 216.
[2] Now part of the Unilever (Anglo-Dutch) concern.
[3] Compulsory schemes under the Coal Mines Act have recently been sanctioned for certain areas.

L

same description largely applies to the other basic industries like iron and steel, engineering, and ship-building. There have been some signs of rationalisation in the Iron and Steel Trades with the formation of the Vickers-Armstrong-Cammell-Laird combine and the Dorman-Long-Bolckow-Vaughan project. More recently we have heard of the big scheme by which Messrs. Stewart and Lloyds are to create at Corby in the North-amptonshire iron ore area steel works on the Bessemer process to cover every operation from the extraction of ore to the despatch, of finished tubes. The finance is to be provided through the Bankers' Industrial Development Company. The same financing company is supporting the Lancashire Steel Corporation with better hopes of success than attended the Lancashire Cotton Corporation.

Hence, in this country, although the progress of rationalisation is as yet hesitating, and the very conception runs counter to some of our national prejudices in favour of traditional custom, rule of thumb, and 'muddling through,' the movement is gaining ground. It is significant that among our most flourishing industries to-day are those which have had the advantage of starting out with up-to-date lay-out and technical equipment— the chemical trades, the artificial silk industry and the motor car industry. In these we find not only relatively high profits and wages, but also a low rate of unemployment.

The Anti-Waste Movement.

In the United States, where, as we have seen, Scientific Management had its origin in the eighties, another feature of rationalisation policy has made conspicuous progress. That is to be seen in the anti-waste movement which received its main impetus from the Hoover Report on *Waste in Industry* prepared in 1921 for the Federated American Engineering Societies. Here attention was drawn to numerous forms of waste—from unemployment during depressions; from speculation and overproduction in booms; from labour turnover; from labour conflicts; from intermittent failure of transportation of supplies of fuel and power; from excessive seasonal operation; from lack of standardisation; from loss in processes and materials and so on.

Four main causes were classified:

> " (a) Low production caused by faulty management of materials, plant, equipment, and men;
> (b) Interrupted production, caused by idle men, idle materials, idle plant, idle equipment;
> (c) Restricted production intentionally caused by owners, management, and labour;
> (d) Lost production caused by ill-health, physical defects, and industrial accidents."

The statistics of estimated waste shewed some remarkable features. For example in the men's clothing industry a total of 63.78 per cent. of all possible waste was found to exist, as an average, over all the plants investigated. Further, the proportion of waste due to management was found to exceed by overwhelming amounts the proportion due to labour.

Since the issue of the Hoover Report the progress made in the elimination of waste has been such as to warrant the description—" one of the most astonishing transformations in economic history."[1] This transformation was largely brought about by the energy of Mr. Hoover himself in his capacity as Secretary of Commerce. The progress shewed itself at the following points:

> " The improvement of transport and reduction of loss by breakages and delay;
> The elimination of unnecessary intermediary agents in distribution and sale;

---

[1] Johnston. *Citizenship in the Industrial World*, p. 82.

The avoidance of merely wasteful and ignorant competition ;

The improvement of statistical services, so that manufacturers might be better able to adjust output to the current state of the market."

The spread of ' simplified practice,' or " the reduction of variety in sizes, dimensions, and immaterial differences in everyday commodities."[1]

Finally, the spread of ' standardisation,' or the devising of standard specifications for all kinds of engineering products, with the object of combining the highest degree of quality and suitability for the purpose to be served.

Of the two last points something more may be said. ' Simplification ' means the negative elimination of unnecessary variations, while standardisation means the positive regulation of desirable standards. We have already discussed the possible dangers attaching to the spread of simplified practice and standardisation and seen little reason to fear undue uniformity or restriction of choice from the steps that have hitherto been taken.[2]

For evidence we have only to look at the list of results of the application of simplified practice to various commodities that is reproduced from a report of Mr. Hoover's in the Balfour Committee Report on *Factors in Industrial and Commercial Efficiency*. The list is at once impressive and unalarming. For example, the number of sizes or varieties of shovels and spades was reduced from 4,460 to 384 ; of face bricks from 38 to 1, of common bricks from 44 to 1 ; of blackboard slates from 251 to 25 ; of milk bottles from 49 to 9 ; of paper bags from 6,280 to 4,700 ; of blankets from 78 to 12, of order forms from thousands to 1, and so on. Mr. Hoover estimated the savings to American manufacturers from the application of his

---

[1] Meakin, *op. cit.*, p. 152.   [2] See p. 33, *supra*.

recommendations at upwards of 600,000,000 dollars annually.[1]

The movement has spread to other countries, and a report of the International Labour Office on *The Social Aspects of Rationalisation* (1931) records developments in Germany, Russia, France, Czechoslovakia, Switzerland and Austria.   In Czechoslovakia, for example, the number of types of railway rails was reduced from 43 to 7, the types of iron pipes for water and gas from 7,854 to 1,336, of screws from 2,300 to 220, of belts from 3,600 to 600, etc.[2] In Great Britain also the movement is progressing. The British Standards Committee under the Board of Trade has been negotiating standardised timber requirements with a view to implementing the agreements reached at the Ottawa Conference, and the British Standards Institution has drawn up specifications and ' yard-sticks ' for application to many industrial materials and products.

That in the sphere of organisation there is room for improvement is shewn by the fact that the American Standardisation Committee discovered that there were 25 organisations working on standardisation in the electrical industry alone, and that most of them were overlapping.[3]

The application of simplified practice and standardisation obviously provides a stimulus both to mass-production and to horizontal cartels and selling arrangements.

> " In mass-production, standardisation is the basis, framework and method of the machine process, for all machine dimensions and process characteristics are measured for service." " Without standardisation mass-production is impossible."[4]

[1] *I.L.O. Report* (Series B., No. 18) on *The Social Aspects of Rationalisation*, p. 62.

[2] *I.L.O. Report*, p. 60.

[3] *Balfour Report on Factors in Industrial and Commercial Efficiency*, p. 286.

[4] Cited in *I.L.O. Report*, p. 61.

The development of the moving assembly line in the motor car industry and in similar mass-production works shews what can be achieved by subdivision of processes. Mr. Ford's description of 'continuous flow' may serve as an illustration, though further mechanical developments eliminating some of the more monotonous process operations have taken place since it was written.

" In the chassis assembling are 45 separate operations on stations. The first men fasten four mud-guard brackets to the chassis-frame ; the motor arrives on the 10th operation and so on in detail. Some men do only one or two small operations, others do more. The man who places a part does not fasten it—this part may not be fully in place until after several operations later. The man who puts in a bolt does not put on the nut ; the man who puts on a nut does not tighten it. In operation No. 34 the budding motor gets its gasoline ; it has previously received lubrication ; on operation No. 44 the radiator is filled with water, and on operation No. 45 the car drives out on the John R. Street.

" Every piece of work in the shop moves ; it may move on hooks on overhead chains going to assembly in the exact order in which the parts are required ; it may travel on a moving platform, or it may go by gravity, but the point is that there is no lifting or trucking of anything other than materials. . . . No workman has anything to do with moving or lifting anything."[1]

Mr. Ford also boasts of other triumphs in the avoidance of waste.

" We put more machinery per square foot of floor and space than any other factory in the world—every foot of space not used carries an overhead expense. . . .

[1] *My Life and Work,* p. 82 *et seq.*

Yet there is all the room needed—no man has too much room and no man has too little room."[1]

In his later book *Moving Forward* he describes various experiments in the utilisation of scrap. Out of the sweepings alone it is estimated that he nets 600,000 dollars a year. At the new Dagenham works in this country he is making use of fuel provided by London's refuse. Transportation charges are saved by distributing assembly stations all over the United States, as well as in other parts of the world. The elaboration of departmental officials and excessive organisation that goes along with some ' efficiency ' schemes are avoided by Ford as ornamental wastage.

But in spite of his heroic endeavours to eliminate waste in space, materials and staff, Mr. Ford has not apparently paid the same attention to the waste represented by labour turnover. Moreover, although he claims to be eliminating the number of monotonous and unskilled operations,[2] his methods of management are open to the objection that the ' speeding-up ' involved means a subjection of the workers to nervous strain that is liable to wear them out prematurely. And if that be so, it means a waste of the most precious of all the factors in production—human life and personality. That mass-production may be able to find a place for the blind, the deaf and dumb, or the deformed or crippled[3] may be reckoned to its credit ; but if it results in premature decay, or in a crippling of the mind among workers who entered young and fresh and vigorous in all their powers, it would stand condemned. I do not say that this result either does or must follow from its adoption ; but I have in mind cases that have been brought to my attention, as well as the statement of an observer in an English mass-production factory (not a Ford concern) : " The workers

<hr>

[1] *op. cit.*, p. 90.   [2] See p. 50, *supra*.
[3] See *My Life and Work*, p. 107 *et seq.*

have no interest in sport, books or theatres, only rest appeals to them."

Technological Unemployment.

But a still more frequent charge against the policy of rationalisation than that of the strain to which the workers are subjected is the charge that it leads to ' over-production ' and unemployment. It is commonly feared that since the policy of rationalisation involves the scrapping of unproductive undertakings and obsolete equipment and the installation of machinery that requires a considerably reduced personnel, the consequences must be a permanent increase of unemployment. It is agreed that there is bound to be a large displacement of workers in the first stage of rationalisation and that measures are required for dealing with displaced employees during the transition period. But although the ' short-run effect ' of temporary technological unemployment is inevitable, it is questionable whether the ' long-run effect ' of permanent technological unemployment is equally inevitable.[1]

The displacement may arise either from a diminution of the total labour force or from the substitution of female labour for male labour. The latter is a frequent occurrence, and is illustrated by a story told by one of my informants, an electrical wireman, who was unemployed (but only for three months) as a result of the installation of a machine that could be worked by semi-skilled cheap female labour.

> " We stood admiring a new machine, my foreman and I. How I delighted in the marvellous ingenuity and complexity of this child of man's brain, this machine. . . . The foreman, too, was enthusiastic—' Why, a girl could work this,' says he. And before the week was out, she *did*, and I didn't ! "

[1] *I.L.O. Report,* p. 263.

In the Hans Renold works at Manchester the proportion of women to men rose in the period between 1913 to 1927 from 31 per cent. to 100 per cent. The firm was employing in 1927 50 more persons than in 1913, the male clerical staff had increased, but the number of semi-skilled and unskilled men had fallen off considerably. An interesting feature, however, is the stability in the number of skilled craftsmen (250 in both 1913 and 1927).[1]

The displacement of workers from mechanised industries may lead to the displacement of other workers whose places are taken by the previously displaced applicants, and so a series of shiftings will result, exaggerating for the time the volume of unemployment. Moreover, the displacement and absorption of labour may go on at different rates over a considerable period of time.

" Moreover, the decline in some industries involves changes of work and of residence which most workers are generally reluctant to make. Finally, even if labour is ultimately transferred and absorbed, it is frequently to a job which pays a lower wage, and which is less satisfactory than the one which is left. It follows, therefore, that while a given set of workers may not be permanently unemployed because of technical progress, there is likely to be a transitional period of unemployment of considerable length, and that more workers will be lower paid at the new jobs they find than at those they left."[2]

But while technological displacement is thus seen to be a serious consequence of rationalisation, new demands for labour also come into being, apart from the obvious stimulation given to the constructional and equipment industries. Mr. Ford claims not only that the numbers of the employees in his concern have increased despite displacements, but also that their products " have made

<hr>

[1] *I.L.O. Report*, p. 238.   [2] *I.L.O. Report*, p. 264.

at least 10 or 20 times as much employment outside of our company as they have in it."[1] The demand on outside industry is not only for materials, parts, services, supply, and sales, but also for the commodities required by the highly paid employees in the undertaking.

In this country there is no evidence of a general displacement of labour consequent on mechanisation, and it would appear that unemployment is more serious where there is not technological displacement than where there is. There is a tendency to ascribe to mechanisation unemployment that is actually caused by other factors —especially those connected with the world depression, the post-war problems of debts and reparations, and the collapse of credit.

" Though in some manufacturing trades machinery appears to be displacing men this is not true of industry and commerce in general, and it is incorrect to say that no economic processes can ever find remunerative work for displaced men. While in manufacturing industries the number actually employed between 1924 and 1929 increased about proportionately to population, the numbers employed in building, transport, distribution, and services increased from 3,549,000 to 4,148,000, well in excess of population growth. Clearly the greater the output from manufacturing industry as a result of mechanisation, the greater is the number of persons required to sell or serve that increased output, since this cannot usually be done mechanically."[2]

Professor Sargent Florence's view is supported by the figures published in the Ministry of Labour *Gazette* for November, 1932, giving the changes that have taken place in the occupation of the insured population of the ages between 16 and 64 in recent years. Mr. Laurence

[1] *Moving Forward*, p. 74.
[2] Professor Sargent Florence in a letter to *The Times*, October 29th, 1932.

Cadbury argues that these figures confirm the view that :

> " Machinery is not inevitably producing an increasing number of men for whom an occupation cannot be found, or causing an over-production of goods for which there is no market. World depression does not make the present a very favourable moment for comparisons. Even so, over the last five years, we find that a long list of trades show increases in the numbers of their insured workpeople ; the distributive trades . . . giving the greatest increase of over 390,000.
>
> " But what is perhaps more to the point, trades where the mechanical development has been particularly in evidence also show that an increase in the numbers occupied has coincided with increased output per head."[1]

The two factors that may serve to compensate in the long run for the displacement of labour are the lowering of real costs consequent on rationalisation and the additional purchasing power arising either from the cheaper price of commodities or from a considered policy of high wages.

In the meanwhile there are four obstacles to the realisation of these gains—economic nationalism and the policy of high tariffs, restriction of output and the artificial buttressing of prices, the confusion of uncontrolled currency and credit policies, and the lack of information as to the elasticity and movement of demand. It is clear that these obstacles can only be removed by international measures for the freeing of international trade, scientific regulation of output, the control of currency and credit, and the supply of information as to world movements of demand. At present there is little hope of advance in these directions.

It is manifest that there is no real ' over-production '

[1] *The Times*, Dec. 1st, 1932.

in the world to-day, and that the defect is in our system of distribution. The ' gluts ' of which complaint is made only exist " in relation to the restricted purchasing demand in the market."[1] " It is the aqueduct which must be made capable of carrying the available supplies ; and not the supplies which must be restricted to the carrying capacity of an insufficient aqueduct."[2]

Mr. J. A. Hobson has been persistently pointing out for many years that " our malady is one of distribution of income,"[3] and rationalisation as it advances is driving home this truth. We are confronted to-day not with a failure of " *consuming* power, i.e., all actual and potential human powers to consume goods and services," but with a failure of " purchasing power, which means the effective demand that people are in fact able to exercise as buyers in the market."[4]

Mass-production requires to be balanced by *mass-consumption.*

> " The history of the nineteenth century might be written mainly in terms of the marvels of large-scale production. It is for us to begin to write the history of the twentieth century in terms of *large-scale consumption.*[5]

To attain this end no doubt international measures such as I have already mentioned are required, but specially

> " the international regulation of *certain* commodities, based upon careful expert study of the elasticity of demand for various primary products, and designed to prevent excessive production, gluts, and the economic paralysis which follows the consequent collapse of prices. . . . In order to be successful as a

---

[1] Henderson. *Economic Consequences of Power Production*, p. 67.
[2] *Ibid.*, p. 65.
[3] *Rationalisation and Employment*, p. 73.
[4] Plummer. *The World in Agony*, p. 38.
[5] Plummer. *op. cit.*, p. 66.

stimulant of purchasing power a high wage policy needs to be not only *generally extended* throughout the world's industries, but *supported* by high purchasing power widely diffused among the agricultural producers of the world."[1]

Here we see the importance of raising the standard of life in non-industrial and more ' backward ' countries and of promoting the efforts of the International Labour Office to secure agreements upon measures affecting hours, wages and working conditions.

The necessity of a policy of high wages may well be the mother of invention.

" Professor Lujo Brentano, in a brochure entitled *Der Ansturm gegen den Achtstundentag* (the attack on the eight-hour day), published in 1923, recalls the declaration made by the American Schönhof more than thirty years earlier, with regard to the effects of high wages and short hours on the awakening of the spirit of invention in America : ' We are inventors by compulsion.' "[2]

So rationalisation may well come to provide the solution of its own problems. We are coming to the point where rationalisation policies must themselves be rationalised on a world scale. If this further development can be brought about, with the aim kept ever in the forefront of promoting a standard of life and leisure that will expand the purchasing power of the peoples of the world, we need have no fear for the future. The immensely increased productivity that machinery puts at our disposal may be utilised to provide a fuller and more leisured life for all. International Labour has declared itself as opposed " not to rationalisation as such, but to the abuses arising from it under the capitalist system," and a Joint Commission of the International

---

[1] Plummer. *op. cit.*, p. 72. (The italics are his.)
[2] *I.L.O. Report*, p. 96.

Federation of Trade Unions and the Labour and Socialist International agreed unanimously to a resolution outlining the safeguards under which rationalisation might be transformed " from a source of unemployment and overwork into a source of well-being."

The resolution urges the following points :

" (1) That rationalisation is not a matter for employers only, since in its operation it may at any time bring about displacement of labour. For this reason the right of Trade Unions to be consulted regarding proposed changes in the methods or conditions of employment or in the distribution of labour should be recognised and machinery for this purpose should be provided, thereby safeguarding the interests of the workers and preventing any scheme of rationalisation from intensifying their exploitation.

" (2) That in order to mitigate as far as possible the effects of rationalisation upon employment and in order to facilitate the changes, the benefits arising from improved technique and organisation should be made immediately available for reducing the hours of work and increasing the real wages of the workers. Unless by raising the real wages of the workers there is sufficient purchasing power in the hands of the people to absorb the commodities produced, unemployment will increase.

(3) That provision should be made for paying adequate unemployment benefits through insurance systems or otherwise, without restriction of time, to persons thrown out of employment. This should apply to all workers, including manual and non-manual workers.

(4) Industry considers it necessary to maintain and improve its plant and equipment. Many firms therefore create reserves not only for depreciation but also for the purpose of replacing plant by more modern types

before it is worn out. It is necessary that industry should pay as much regard to the human element as to plant and equipment and that technical progress should not involve hardship to the workers concerned. Industry should take all financial responsibility possible for the alleviation of the hardship caused by the substitution of machinery for human labour. This responsibility should come before the responsibility of industry to its shareholders.

(5) Finally, governments should use to the fullest extent all means at their disposal to find employment for displaced workers under conditions at least equal to those previously enjoyed by them, or fit them for work in other employment."[1]

Organised labour is naturally suspicious of methods of rationalisation which fail to provide for the consultation and co-operation of the Trade Unions in the working out of the changes required. But if this can be secured, if the interests of displaced workers are safeguarded, and if the benefits of more efficient organisation are made a means of raising the workers' standard of life and leisure, rationalisation will be welcomed.

The problem of production has been solved, but it remains to solve the problem of distribution, the distribution of purchasing power and the distribution of working time. And then to the problem of labour will be added the problem of leisure.

[1] *Reports and Proceedings of Fourth Congress of the Labour and Socialist International* (Vienna, 1931).

CHAPTER XIII

IT is significant that the word 'leisure' and the word 'licence' have a common origin in the Latin verb *licēre*= 'to be permitted'—to possess freedom of action in a certain sphere. A 'licence' is a permission to exercise freedom in certain matters. 'Licentiousness' is misuse of that freedom. The connexion with 'leisure' is not without significance. Leisure is the time permitted to us to act freely, the time that is at our own disposal, to be spent in our own way in activities of our own choosing. The opposite of leisure then is not activity but industry or business—the work that must be performed at certain times and according to orders.

Leisure is not necessarily vacant, idle, or unemployed ; its characteristic is that it is employed exactly as we choose and not at the beck and call of others or under the continuous pressure of a disciplined routine. It may be spent fruitfully or mis-spent licentiously, and that is why the leisure problem, though it is seldom spoken of as a problem, is no less important than the labour problem.

Moreover, the two problems are closely inter-related. The interdependence of industry and leisure is shown in three main ways :

(1) The amount of time spent in business determines the amount of time available for leisure. It is significant that we always start from the assumption that the primary and constant factor is the time required for industry and adapt our 'spare' time to that. An Athenian of the fifth century B.C. might have made the equally obvious converse statement that the amount of time spent in leisure

determines the amount of time available for business.

(2) The amount of energy absorbed in business determines the amount of energy available for leisure. Here again, the converse is equally true, and it frequently occurs to us to put it, just because we have come to consider that our best energies should be reserved and preserved for business. For leisure is regarded " as an *interlude* " (the word is significant from its association with ' play ') " in the serious business of life, and as having only the ' instrumental value ' of furnishing rest and refreshment for work."[1]   Dr. Jacks instances the college don who plays golf or takes long walks in his leisure time " with the avowed object of ' keeping himself fit ' for the severer occupations of the study and lecture-room," and the bishop " who indulges of an evening in a quiet game of bridge on the ground, as one of them informs me, that ' it clears his mind and calms his temper for dealing with recalcitrant clergy,' "[2]   A Civil Service clerical officer (a woman of 35) writes to me :   " To be honest my leisure occupations sometimes leave me less than fresh for work." She speaks of golf, skating, occasional dinners and theatres, reading novels or travel books, adult education classes, home upholstery (making cushions, eiderdowns, bedspreads, etc.), running a flat with two friends (cooking and baking one week in three), and on Sundays churchgoing, letter-writing or hiking.

(3) The character of our leisure interests and occupations (or pre-occupations) determines in large measure the character and direction of productive industry, because in our leisure we consume not only time but goods and services.   The improvement in the worker's standard of life made possible by machine industry reacts upon the character of the products of the machine.   For in so far as the worker has higher or increased purchasing power and shorter hours, he has more ' spare cash ' to spend and also

[1] Dr. L. P. Jacks in *The Observer*, Sept. 25th, 1932.
[2] *Ibid.*

M

more ' spare time ' in which to spend it.   Consequently he makes demands not only on the ' staple ' industries but on the ' leisure ' industries.   As this process continues, the balance between ' staple ' and ' luxury ' trades, and especially between agriculture and other forms of industry will still further be disturbed.

" Mechanisation, both in industry and agriculture, enormously increases the output per man.   Industry can, within limits, increase its market correspondingly. There is no limit to what man will buy if he has the money; the pedestrian will advance to cycles, the cyclist to automobiles, and a taste for radios and gramophones and similar luxuries recently unknown can develop indefinitely.   But man's appetite is not similarly elastic."[1]

With these points in mind, let us examine man's attitude to leisure, the ways in which he regards it, and the ways in which he occupies it.

Holidays and Work Days.

One of the biggest differences between ancient and modern civilisation (and probably also between eastern and western civilisation) is in the attitude to work and leisure, and in the proportion of workdays to holidays.[2] Partly it is no doubt a question of climate.   Modern civilisation is predominantly a Northern and Western civilisation, while the ancient civilisations were of the East and South.   The Northern climate is more conducive to continuous physical and mental activity.   At any rate it would appear that in primitive societies life was more ' leisurely ' and work more intermittent.[3]   The ancient civilisations, which were nearer to primitive conditions, preserved something of the intermittent attitude in their

---

[1] Salter.   *Recovery*, p. 34.   (cf. note at end of this chapter).
[2] Delisle Burns.   *Leisure in the Modern World* (*passim*).
[3] *Supra*, p. 30.

arrangement of work, and it is probable that the dislike of more regular and exacting work and its restriction to native serfs or foreign slaves was prompted not by the desire to be idle but by the desire to be leisurely.[1] It is significant that though there is a Greek word for ' work,' there is no word for business except a negative term meaning ' lack of leisure ' ($\dot{\alpha}\sigma\chi o\lambda\acute{\iota}\alpha$). Leisure was the positive term ($\sigma\chi o\lambda\acute{\eta}$), and it has often been pointed out that it is also the word from which we derive the words ' school ' and ' scholar.'

Time was divided in the ancient world between agriculture and mental and physical culture. Agricultural peasants—whether slave or ' free '—have probably always been deprived of adequate leisure in comparison with either nomadic peoples or town workers. These enjoyed frequent popular and religious festivals or holidays (holy days).

" In Ancient Egypt, it seems, holidays amounted to one fifth of the year ; in ancient Athens there were fifty to sixty days of festival in the year ; and at Tarentum in the days of its prosperity there were more holidays than working days. In ancient Rome about one-third of the days of the year were *nefasti*, unlucky for work ; and in the later Empire the ' games ' and other festivals were largely extended."[2]

According to Sombart, Western Europe in the fourteenth century contained " hundreds of communities which averaged from 160 to 180 holidays a year."[3] Henry VIII in 1536 suppressed a number of superfluous holy-days. Both Sundays and holy-days had frequently been violated before, but from the time of the Reformation public sanction is given to their disregard. We must probably ascribe the beginning of modern industrial

---

[1] The disparagement of the " vulgar crafts " was also due to the dislike of " indoor " occupations. See p. 30, *supra*.

[2] Delisle Burns, *op. cit.*, p. 190.

[3] Cited by Chase. *Men and Machines*, p. 183.

civilisation in large part to the Puritan movement with its emphasis on continuous industry as a moral duty and its disparagement of the arts and amusements of leisure.[1] The Industrial Revolution wrought a further change in men's habits of life.   Work became more rigidly organised and disciplined when the factory supplanted the domestic workshop, and the machine and not the craftsman's will dictated the speed of work.   In the interests of profits the fullest use of the machinery required a long working day which left little or no time or energy for leisure.   Just as Aristotle invented the excuse for slavery that some men are " by nature living tools " and " have a capacity for belonging to someone else," so the early capitalist employers invented the excuse that some men are " incapable of profiting by leisure and fit only for the long discipline of factory hours."   The Hammonds declare that this was the prevailing view among employers in the early nineteenth century, and quote a statement of the year 1818 to the following effect :—

" All experience proves that in the lower orders the deterioration of morals increases with the quantity of unemployed time of which they have the command."[2]

It was convenient to the employer to believe that

" Satan finds some mischief still
For idle hands to do."

So holidays came to be reduced to a minimum, and although the festivals of Christmas, Easter, and Whitsuntide remain festivals of the church and public holidays, they stand out from the rest of the working year in even greater contrast than when there were more frequent festivals.

" We have now, by a series of accidents, reduced the number of Greek–Roman festivals and preserved the

---

[1] cf. Tawney.   *Religion and the Rise of Capitalism.*
[2] *The Town Labourer*, p. 49.

regularity of the Hebraic tradition ; so that we have in the Western world about sixty days of public holiday in a year—that is to say, only about half the number that was common in most highly civilised societies in the past."[1]

Dr. Delisle Burns has elsewhere pointed out the significance of the modern institution of ' Bank Holiday.' Speaking of the festival in the Middle Ages and in non-industrial countries to-day, he says :—

" The holiday which is a festival is not a mere rest or interval in work. It is an expending of energy upon other objects : and indeed the working days are conceived to be for the sake of the holiday. In such festivals there is communal enjoyment, and the art of consumption is expressed in song and dance. These festivals died out with the coming of the industrial era, but it was found that the rhythms which they had allowed in life had been useful and re-invigorating. The other effects were unnoticeable, for they were not calculable in exchange values. In order to obtain, therefore, a re-invigoration, the reformers re-introduced the intervals in work, but no longer as festivals. Significantly the intervals were called ' bank ' holidays, and they were thus made part of the economic life."[2]

It was in 1871 that Sir John Lubbock secured the establishment of these ' Bank Holidays,' when even the bankers cease from troubling, and the bank clerks are at rest.

It is generally recognised that the gradual reduction of hours of work during the last half century brought some measure of relief from the strain of industry to the actual advantage of both output and quality of work. It is notable that one of the advantages claimed for the Ten Hours Act was that it made clear the distinction between the worker's own time and his master's.

---

[1] Delisle Burns, *op. cit.*, p. 190. [2] *Industry and Civilisation*, p. 214.

The Report of Inspectors of Factories for 1848 says :—

" The worker knows now when the time which he sells is ended, and when his own begins, and by possessing a sure foreknowledge of this, is enabled to pre-arrange his own minutes for his own purposes."

They go on to suggest that the employers also felt the advantage, as they were free to give time to something other than business, and even to a little ' culture,' whereas in former days, " the master had no time for anything but money, the servant had no time for anything but labour."[1]

It is significant that a certain hostility that is sometimes manifested against factory welfare work, especially when it extends to the organisation of the leisure time and interests of the worker, arises from the feeling that is expressed in the words : " I give the employer my work time, why should he want to encroach on my leisure ? "[2]

The Shorter Working Week.

We have described earlier[3] the advantages to the health and vitality of the worker that followed from the progressive shortening of the working day. We may expect the length of the working day or at any rate of the working week to be still further reduced from the eight-hour standard that largely obtains to-day. The late Lord Leverhulme in his evidence before the Health of Munition Workers Committee made his famous pronouncement in favour of a six-hour day.

" When our modern industries are run on a less fatiguing system of say two shifts each of six and a half hours with half an hour off for meals (making six working hours in all per day) the efficiency of the worker by thus avoiding fatigue can be increased by

[1] Cited by Marx in *Capital*, Vol. I, end of ch. viii.
[2] R. M. Fox. *The Triumphant Machine*, p. 12.
[3] Chapter VI.

33 per cent., and consequently as much work can readily be done in six working hours as under present conditions is done in eight."[1]

Since then not only the Ford automobile works and the Bata boot and shoe mass-production factory, but a number of other firms in the United States and Czechoslovakia, have adopted the five-day week of forty-five to forty-eight hours. In the Bata concern the distribution of work days and holidays is now 252 working days, and 113 holidays, including 9 consecutive days of holiday.[2]

It is significant that since the institution in 1889 of May Day as an International Labour Day throughout the world the resolutions that have always been most prominent in the international demonstrations on that day have been in support of an eight-hour day and of a guaranteed period of holidays with pay. Thus one of the oldest and most universal of Spring Festivals has been made the occasion of urging the expansion of the leisure of the workers. Since the Great War and the Great Depression the alarming increase in the numbers of the unemployed throughout the world (rising to-day to thirty millions) has given a new impetus to the demand of labour for shorter hours in industry. The American Recovery Campaign has been largely concentrated on securing a reduction of hours throughout American industry. We have already quoted the resolution of the Joint Commission of the International Federation of Trade Unions and the Labour and Socialist International urging that the benefits arising from rationalisation " should be made immediately available for reducing the hours of work and increasing the real wages of the worker."[3]

Prophecies are often put forward of the possibilities in the future of an indefinite expansion of leisure for all as a

---

[1] See *Final Report of Health of Munition Workers' Committee*, 1918. (Cd. 9065.)

[2] *I.L.O. Report, Social Aspects of Rationalisation*, p. 153.

[3] *Supra*, p. 170.

result of the further mechanisation of industry. Bertrand Russell looks forward to a four-hour day :—

> " If we could abolish wars and armaments and advertisements and the waste of commercial competition, we could all subsist comfortably on about four hours work a day. . The rest of our time ought to be free, and education ought to prepare us for an intelligent use of the twenty hours a day during which we should be left to our own initiative."[1]

Mr. Cecil Chisholm prophesies a four- or five-day week with a working day of six to eight hours by 1950, and looking further ahead expects a three-day and a two-day week to follow, until ultimately one day a week may be reached.[2]

In the meantime how far is even a moderate expansion of leisure adequate compensation for unsatisfactory work ? The author of *The Triumphant Machine* holds that even a short period of repetition work is bound to have serious consequences for the worker, and that its influence must inevitably carry over into his leisure, resulting " in a ' feed and speed ' outlook on life." For " if a daily dose of poison, however small, is taken, the worker can hardly escape unharmed."[3] Mr. Bernard Shaw, on the other hand, contends that we ought all to contribute " a daily share of service to the community," and that he himself would prefer to contribute it in the form of work that is " as brainlessly mechanical as you can make it."

> " For my two hours or so of obligatory service. let me be as complete a Robot as possible, so that I may do my job without having to turn my mind on to it."[4]

We have seen good reason to suppose that the more mechanical repetition work of the machine-feeder will

---

[1] *Prospects of Industrial Civilisation*, p. 263.
[2] *Vulcan*, p. 70.   [3] p. 23.
[4] Cited by Chisholm, *Vulcan*, p. 72.

increasingly itself be taken over by the machine.[1] The remaining drudgery, and we shall never eliminate every form of drudgery,[2] will be combined with skilled and interesting work, which itself need not occupy more than a portion of the week, leaving the rest of the week for leisure pursuits, such as intellectual or artistic work or outdoor occupations.

The Effect of Work on Leisure.

Already, however, we have gained an amount of leisure that means, at any rate to some types of worker, a considerable space of ' spare time,' and may even constitute something of a problem.   For an eight-hour working day means only a third of the whole day, and a forty-eight hour working week means only a little more than a quarter of a whole week or of a whole year.

In other words, 120 hours of every week and 8 or 9 months a year are not actually spent in work. It may reasonably be objected that a large proportion of this time is taken up in sleeping, eating meals, and going to and from one's work. Rest indeed, complete relaxation of both mind and body, is a rhythmical necessity of man's nature which demands from five to eight hours out of the twenty-four, and restricts the period of waking leisure. Meals again, and recreation in the form of physical exercise or the various kinds of play, are essential means of restoring and re-creating body and mind. But allowing eight hours a day or four months in the year for rest and sleep, and three hours a day or one and a half months a year for meals, we still have over two months for leisure activities. It will be objected, and again with good reason, that these two months do not come ' on end,' but in broken snatches and fragments, in odd hours and half-hours.   It is indeed one of the arguments in favour of the five-day week that it provides a longer week-end of continuous leisure.   Mr. Wells' William Clissold wished

[3] *Supra,* p. 96.   [2] *Supra,* p. 81.

that the people who invented the week had invented it longer and larger, and with more than one day of rest at the end of it, and would have preferred to work " in spells of six to eight days of steady work followed by three or four days of play, gossip, laughter and rest." There are many people who would like, not indeed perhaps a longer week, but certainly a longer week-end.

Moreover, the nature of the work of a great many workers still exacts a toll of their physical and mental energy which leaves them with little inclination or capacity for turning to good purpose either the daily fragments or the week-end spaces of leisure time. A working-class student whom I approached to supply evidence for the late Master of Balliol's Adult Education Report to the Ministry of Reconstruction (1918), told me that after his day's work " physical exhaustion has usually reached a point where no advantage can be taken of educational opportunities." Many of the workers whom I have more recently consulted on the point make similar complaints. A miner says :—

> " My work incapacitates me for the full enjoyment of my leisure time. At the conclusion of my day's work I do not feel like indulging in much exercise, either physical or mental. Consequently, much of my leisure time, except for an occasional visit to a cinema, attendance at W.E.A. classes during the winter months, and occasional reading, is frittered away in lounging aimlessly about."

The 'brain' worker has indeed a marked advantage over the 'manual' worker, in that he can often turn with relief and zest to physical activity, whereas the 'manual' worker cannot turn as readily or gladly to mental activity ; for, in the first place many kinds of 'manual' work are falsely so called because they require a considerable degree of dexterity, alertness and decision involving more brain activity than some forms of clerical work which are largely automatic ;[1] and, in the second place, physical fatigue, as we have seen,[2] affects the nervous system and the brain, and incapacitates for arduous mental effort.

A cotton-spinner writes :—

" My work does sap energy out of me. I suppose this is because of the heat. I do not feel much like strenuous exercise in the evenings."

But some kinds of ' manual ' work leave much more energy for leisure than others. A worker who has been employed both as a farm labourer and as a gardener and chauffeur tells me that farming left him generally so tired that he had " no inclination for enjoyment, only just to rest and prepare for next day," while after gardening and driving

" I could take " (he says) " more interest in social affairs in the evening, but usually not of a physical nature. I was very fond of reading, attending lectures, classes for adult students, and wireless groups. . . . With a physical occupation I got the most pleasure in my leisure time from doing something of a mental nature, not requiring any further physical exertion."

Work that induces either physical fatigue or nervous tension largely accounts for the worker's tendency to resort in leisure hours to amusements that titillate and mildly entertain a passive mind rather than to those which make exacting demands on his attention. The music hall and the ' pictures ' owe their excess of popularity over the theatre and the concert not merely to cheaper prices nor to ' low-brow ' tastes, but to the tired bodies and jaded nerves of the audience.

A smith's striker says :—

" I must admit that furnace work has sometimes compelled me to go to the cinema because I have felt physically tired and mentally indolent, and wanted only

---

[1] cf. *supra*, p. 40.   [2] *Supra*. p. 57.

to sink into a comfortable seat and be entertained with a minimum of effort on my part."

A miner says :—

" When one considers the extent of monotony, suppression and physical fatigue which is the lot of the average colliery worker, it is small wonder that he rushes to entertainments where little intelligence is required, and reading of the lighter kind. This is not always so, and the war conditions (seven-hour day, etc.), which were an improvement, had an influence for the better use of leisure."

We have seen that the conditions of the more mechanised forms of work are apt to replace physical fatigue by nervous tension.[1] This has its peculiar effects on the leisure of the machine-feeder. A worker (aged 36) in a mass-production factory writes :—

" I find my greatest satisfaction in leisure hours in the more arduous and violent pursuits, gardening, hiking, cycling, and till quite recently football. The less strenuous type of game I have no interest in. I spend much time in the social activities of the district, religion, politics, and international organisation, which call for a great deal of energy and effort. To sit down and read books I find boring and I therefore do little. I think this is in a large measure due to the fact that I am (so to speak) tied all day to my machine and there is a desire to give vent to stored up feeling, when one is free to do so. . . . From talk and association with other work people, I would say that much of the lust for out-door games, speeding on the road, and sensationalism of the films, is due to the desire to give vent to pent up feelings of monotony and boredom."

Lack of interest in life and work also often accounts for the resort to forms of excitement like betting and gambling

[1] *Supra*, p. 28.

or to narcotics like alcohol.   Alcohol offers a means of escape and of detachment from wearisome or irksome conditions of life which is eagerly sought by those who want an escape and a dope.   For it is notable that drinking and gambling are alike resorted to by those who are either too tired or too bored to be able to occupy their leisure in more creative forms of interest and enjoyment.   Working class students in Oxford have told me that during their period in College they have lost any desire to gamble or to drink, to which they would normally succumb in their ordinary working life.   Many of them, indeed, had already found that more fruitful leisure interests had driven out such habits, or prevented their adoption.   Mr. Jack Lawson, M.P., a former student of Ruskin College, tells in his fine book *A Man's Life*, how the gambling habit grew " stale with the growth of mental appetite. It ended finally, for the two things would not run together."[1]

The tendencies to gambling and drinking are not merely a question of economic conditions, for the same tendencies are found often in the most extreme excesses among those who are relieved from all economic pressure but are afflicted by an excessive amount of unemployed leisure which they have never learnt to occupy in any fruitful way. This ' leisure class ' has been well analysed by Veblen, who points out two main characteristics, (1) ' conspicuous leisure ' or non-productive consumption of time, involving dependence not only on the productive workers of the world but also on the personal services of a ' vicarious leisure class ' of footmen, lacqueys, and other domestic servants ; (2) conspicuous consumption and ostentatious display of luxury.[2]   To these habits of a ' leisure class ' may be added a tendency to restlessness and futile movement.   Mr. Wells in *William Clissold* describes the ' stratum of futility ' among the prosperous middle-aged.

[1] p. 80.
[2] See *The Theory of a Leisure Class.*

" The activity to escape mental solitude is remarkable. Most of the rushing about in motor-cars is plainly due to that.   The rich, ageing Americans in particular, seem constantly in flight across the Atlantic from something that is always, nevertheless, waiting for them on the other side, whichever side it happens to be.   There would not be all this vehement going to and fro if they were not afraid of something that sought them in the quiet places.   And what else can that something be but just these questions that have confronted us ? ' There is only a little handful of water left now.   What do you mean to do with it ?   What under the stars is the meaning of your life ? '   ' Oh, hell ! ' they say at the first intimation of that whisper, ' Where are we going to to-morrow ? ' "

Dr. L. P. Jacks in the *Hibbert Journal* for January, 1929, draws attention to the same tendency in all quarters to-day :—

" We tend more and more to spend our leisure on the move, like nomads ; seldom in one place for five minutes without wishing to be somewhere else, a want which the waiting motor-car stands ready to satisfy. Our homes, in which we are supposed to rest, are in danger of becoming mere points of departure."

Possibly the increase of gambling among women is partly accounted for by factors producing boredom in their lives.   In the working classes women and girls are employed in the more monotonous forms of machine work both in the factory and the office.   In the middle and upper classes women are finding more leisure because of the improvements in large-scale production of food and clothing,[1] and because of the smaller numbers of the modern family.

" The management of a nursery has never been such a highly skilled job as it is to-day, but it does not go on

[1] Delisle Burns, *op. cit.*, p. 18.

being a job for nearly as long. In almost all families the girls as well as the boys now go to school—the family itself seldom exceeds four—and by about 30 or 35 the modern mother is more or less out of work. The personal life has called her and the urgent demands of the personal life have been satisfied. And now what is she going to do with the rest of her life, the 30 or 40 years which remain ? "[1]

Mr. H. G. Wells, after making this observation, adds the further question : " Is there, after 40, any alternative to bridge ? "

The Employment of Leisure.

Consideration of the habits and standards of a class removed from the necessity of work and supplied with a superabundance of both spare cash and spare time leads one to sound a warning against any social policy which is confined to the demand for increased material prosperity and decreased hours of labour. It becomes increasingly important to accompany the pursuit of higher wages and shorter hours by a process of education which will guide men in the spending of their wealth and in the spending of their leisure. And such education will reflect itself not only in the character of leisure occupations but also in the reaction of the leisure demands of the consumer upon the character of the goods and services which are the objects of production. Dr. L. P. Jacks asks us to examine the goods in the shop windows and the quotations of industrial securities to see " from what quarter the wind mainly blows in our industrial climate. *It blows mainly from the leisure end.*"[2] The ' new ' industries, which supply motors, gramophones, wireless sets and films, are largely ' leisure ' and ' entertainment ' industries.[3] The future of a great part of industry is likely to be bound up

---

[1] Wells. *The Work, Wealth and Happiness of Mankind*, p. 555.
[2] *Hibbert Journal*, January, 1929. His italics.
[3] cf. Delisle Burns, *op. cit.*. chs. 4 & 5.

with the demands which are made not for the staple needs of the meal-table, but for the means of enhancing and beguiling the intervals between meals. Dr. Jacks points out as characteristic of our time the fact that pleasure *buying* has taken the place of pleasure *seeking*, and as Mr. Joad says in *Diogenes : or The Future of Leisure*, we are coming to have " a false notion of entertainment as something for which one pays."[1] It is possible that we are going through a transitional period in which we are experiencing a reaction from conditions in which our appetite for material goods and comforts has been overlong starved and thwarted, and Professor Dewey thinks that we may look forward to " recovery of a sane equilibrium after the so long inhibited appetites have glutted themselves."[2] But we have to remember that a younger generation is growing up which knows nothing of the former inhibitions and prohibitions and is acquiring standards of taste and enjoyment which it will be difficult to dislodge.

Meanwhile a problem immediately confronting us is that of the unfortunate class of unemployed who are doomed to enforced and *unprovisioned* leisure, because they have spare time but no spare cash. What they ask is to be occupied. It is not enough to provide the means of entertainment and recreation, though these have their place, for recreation as ordinarily understood does not yield the satisfactions of steady employment, even if the livelihood be assured. Men tire of recreation, as we know from the older ' leisured class ' of the unemployed persons of ' independent means,' who find " to sport as tedious as to work."

The irony of our present situation is that thousands of people with absorbing hobbies have insufficient leisure to enjoy or pursue them to the full, while thousands more have over-much leisure, but are baffled what to do with it.

[1] p. 11.
[2] In *Whither Mankind ?* p. 325.

The two-fold need of the time is a distribution of purchasing power that shall enable the mass of people to employ each other's industrial skills and services, and a distribution of trained and " provisioned leisure "[1] that shall enable the mass of people to ' employ themselves ' when they are not otherwise employed.[2]

[1] Henderson. *Economic Consequences of Power Production*, p. 212.

[2] Professor Hersch, of the University of Geneva, has pointed out that the decline of the birth-rate in Europe is affecting the age-distribution of the population, and diminishing the proportion of producers in relation to consumers. He argues that, apart from measures affecting the purchasing power of the masses and the hours of labour, " the most important remedy . . . would be a change in the distribution of population and capital among the different branches of economic life." The demand for " staple " goods is relatively inelastic, but the demand for " cultural " goods is infinitely elastic, and " the human energy no longer required for the satisfaction of primary physical needs should be re-enlisted in the service of the mind and spirit." The watchword of the future, he suggests, should be " from quantity to quality." (See *Times* for Sept. 14th, 1933.)

CHAPTER XIV

EDUCATION in all stages is too generally regarded as a means to a career and a livelihood, that is, as an equipment for work ; and too seldom regarded as an equipment for leisure. For if, as we have suggested, the problem of leisure is looming up to-day along with the problem of labour, then education as a preparation for life must take account of the life of leisure as well as of the life of work. For work is a means to other ends than the mere achievement of a livelihood, and it is quite possible to possess a livelihood and still to be without a proper and a reasonable life. Further, the progressive reduction in the hours of labour and corresponding expansion of the margin of leisure goes to make education for leisure of incalculable importance. Leisure provides an opportunity, not only for rest and recreation, but also for the cultivation and enjoyment of those interests which are not satisfied by a man's daily occupation. Moreover, if artistic craftsmanship and the other forms of manual skill are receding under the conditions of machine industry, there is all the more reason to make provision in our leisure time for the pursuit of arts and crafts which will give expression to aptitudes and interests that might otherwise be starved for lack of opportunity. It is a good thing that leisure occupations should supplement and counter-balance the kinds of work that people do, so that intellectual workers, for example, should have hobbies like carpentry or gardening, and 'manual' workers, on the other hand, should be able to turn with zest and profit to reading or writing, for purposes of study or of self-expression. For this reason, among others, it is desirable that the early education of boys and girls should be well balanced between bookish and practical interests. Under the Hadow scheme of educational re-organisation it is intended that children whose capacity and bent appears to be more bookish shall be diverted at 11 plus into a more bookish type of education of the ' Secondary School ' pattern, and that children of more practical capacity and bent shall be diverted into a form of education that shall have at least a practical ' bias,' without being primarily or purely technical or vocational, such as is given in the ' Central Schools.'   But there are reasons for doubting if this is altogether wise.   In the first place who is to decide and how is he to decide that certain boys or girls are predominantly bookish ?   If the break is to be made at 11 plus, I suggest that, although that is a suitable age for transferring children to a post-primary stage of education, it is not a suitable age for classifying them in divisions corresponding to the proposed ' Grammar ' and ' Modern' schools[1]; for it is only in the period of early adolescence— say, from 13 plus or 14 to 16—that interests and proclivities begin to show themselves in any marked or permanent degree.   (This is one of the reasons for the raising of the school-leaving age, for the child of 14 is too young and inexperienced to take the all-important step of entering on an occupation, and is consequently all too often decided by irrelevant or inadequate considerations.)[2]

But in the second place, it is doubtful if a purely bookish type of education is good for the bookish type of child— even if we have found him.   It is even possible that the best type of ' Central ' or ' Modern ' school may be educationally better for all kinds of children than the narrowly bookish type of ' Secondary ' or ' Grammar ' school.   It is the more unfortunate that there is a ten-

---

[1] See Hadow Report on the *Education of the Adolescent.*
[2] See Macrae, *Talents and Temperaments,* for a discussion of the problems of vocational guidance.

dency to provide the better equipment and staffing for the ' Grammar ' school, and so to disfavour the ' Modern ' school and sustain a bad form of social distinction. It were better that all children should pass at 11 plus into schools in which the buildings, equipment and staffing would be of the best ' secondary ' type, but in which varieties of courses, corresponding alike to bookish and to practical interests, should be provided, with opportunity for selection of ' sides,' but not insistence on them or permission of their exclusive pursuit. Let me state briefly the reasons for this view :

(1) It allows the classification of children and their relative specialisation to take place gradually and not at a pre-determined moment in life—and that a moment psychologically premature ;

(2) It gives to all children of all types of capacity and bent the opportunity of acquiring the best of both the more literary and the more practical educational training ;

(3) It avoids the danger of emphasising an undesirable form of social or class distinction ;

(4) In particular, it is not so liable as the Hadow proposal to turn out, on the one hand, a set of boys and girls whose only expectation is that of teaching or clerical work, and, on the other hand, a set whose only expectation is that of ' manual ' work ;

(5) It is designed to develop qualities of adaptability and versatility which are of the greatest importance in modern industry and commerce ;[1]

(6) It is designed to foster leisure interests which are of the highest importance in modern life.

It is the last point that primarily concerns us here.

Dean Inge once said : " The soul is dyed the colour of its leisure thoughts " ; and the most significant test of the education of a people is to be found in the way in which

---

[1] cf. *supra*, p. 50; also *Report on Education for Salesmanship*, p. 38.

they spend their leisure.   More and more I am impressed by the amount of creative ability that is only too often smothered by ordinary schooling, and certainly by the ordinary routine of life and work. Twenty years' experience of teaching adult students, in Tutorial classes, in the residential work of Ruskin College, and in its large Correspondence Department, has made this unmistakably clear to me.   The daily post-box of the College bears witness to this widespread longing for creative expression. Poems and short stories and plays come from postmen and telegraph clerks, miners and railwaymen, printers and mechanics, and from every type of worker, both ' manual ' and clerical.   During the past year my correspondence students have included steel workers, clerks, postal workers, miners, printers, weavers, teachers, journalists, tram conductors, a cook-general, a dental surgeon, a nurse, a soldier on the North West Frontier, a telegraph clerk in South Africa, a farmer's wife and a retired music-teacher. Here is a multitude of men and women feeling after some means of expression that shall satisfy a need that has something of the quality of an appetite, which disturbs its possessor as long as it is unappeased.   Adult education exists to save people from the boredom and dissatisfaction of an empty mind and a meaningless and vapid life.   It is significant that one often hears of men who retire from business and shortly afterwards are dead.   I hazard the assertion that many of them die because they cannot think of anything else to do.   Contrast these men with those who only ask for more leisure from their occupations to follow up their absorbing pre-occupations ; men who have cultivated hobbies varying from handicrafts to gardening, from painting to play-writing or philosophy.   I once had a pupil at a Summer School of the Workers' Educational Association who was employed in the Chatham dockyard, and due to retire on his pension in two years' time (he was then 58).   He chose to study psychology in order to follow up his interest in his fellow-workmen, and especially the younger people. Among my correspondence students is a retired music teacher of 63 who is a keen gardener, and is studying both literature and philosophy. A still more notable example of well occupied leisure throughout a long life is that of Mr. W. S. Rogers of Falmouth who kindly allows me to quote from the unpublished manuscript of a book called *My Hobbies and Some Recollections.* He has recorded his hobbies because he has noted

> " the sad fact that so many of my contemporaries, who, like myself, had abandoned the turmoil of life to settle down to a life of ease, were at sea in their retirement, like rudderless ships, with no interest to keep their minds active, and no occupation to exercise their muscles, with the result that their lives were colourless and in some cases a burden to them. Not so in my case, for at 78 I find myself still young and able to enjoy life with as much zest as I did at 40."

Mr. Rogers has lived a full and varied life. His father, was a veterinary surgeon, and also an artist of some ability, and was acquainted with many artists, including Landseer and George and Robert Cruikshank. He gave his boy when he was 13 years old a box of tools of good quality, some of which he still uses after 60 years. The father died when the boy was 17, but he had instilled in him a love of natural history, of drawing and of craftsmanship. The boy was educated at Berkhamsted Grammar School, and later at King's College, London, where he studied applied science. He was divided between art and engineering, but decided on the latter, and served the electrical engineering firm of Siemens Bros. for whom he travelled to Brazil to lay cables, and to Turkey to instal searchlights for the Turkish Government. He also had a share in English railway construction, and carried out some of the earliest electrical installations in English ships and theatres. All this time he pursued art in his leisure moments, and for a time he abandoned engineering and took to poster-designing and garden-designing side by side, with art photography as a further interest. Between 50 and 60 (when he retired) he was engaged as advertisement manager to a chemical works. He has written several books : *A Book of the Poster*, *Villa Gardens*, *Garden Planning*, and the *Gramophone Handbook*, as well as unpublished verses, short stories, detective tales, and film scenarios. Among his collections are Brazilian butterflies, British mosses and fungi, pictures, bric-à-brac, and furniture. Among the hobbies which he still pursues in his old age are painting, photography, work in pewter, silver and enamel, carving and engraving, fishing (he makes his own tackle), garden designing and construction, and much light cabinet work. When over 70 he designed and made a new type of cabinet gramophone. Among the many inventions which he has produced are a hand camera an ingenious tobacco-pipe, a vacuum cleaner, a picture-hook, and a mirror pivoting device.[1]

" At the moment " (he writes to me), " I am working on a loom for domestic use that can stand on the table and produce a web 13 inches wide. It promises to be a success and being almost automatic it will simplify home weaving."

Of this astonishing record he writes with modest enthusiasm.

" I don't suggest " (he says), " that everyone should tackle so many arts and crafts. It was my good fortune to be possessed of a faculty that enabled me to grasp any process new to me, and attain to some degree of skill in practising it. The main purpose of this book, however, is not so much to glorify my own achievements as to convey to the reader some idea of the vast amount of interest that is created by the study of the many arts and crafts available to those who seek recreation for their

---

[1] See *supra*, p. 125.

spare time, and to offer them some encouragement to adopt one or other of them as a resource and relaxation from the more serious business of making a livelihood. The man immersed in commercial pursuits is none-the-less a good man of business because he follows a hobby when divorced from his office routine. Moreover, he would not be precluded from playing his game of golf or from indulging in outdoor pursuits. I have never allowed my hobbies to obsess me to the extent of curtailing my exercise, for I have indulged in much walking, mountain climbing, fishing and other open air pastimes. And throughout my life I have given my best to the business with which I have been connected. Now, in the autumn of life, in my retirement, I can give free rein to such pursuits as fancy dictates for the time being, and by doing so I believe that I am warding off the decrepitude that comes with old age."

Mr. Rogers supports the contention advanced above that education should be of wide range and not too narrowly bookish.

" Always it has seemed to me that an educational system omits an important subject when it finds no room for instruction in those sciences that have to do with animal and plant life. Besides the equipment calculated to fit a man for commercial or professional life, he should be furnished with knowledge that will create resources for intellectual expansion, and such as may serve to fill his leisure with some engrossing study to act as a counterpoise to the more strenuous work of money-making."

Mr. Rogers tells of other men of his acquaintance, many of them " in humble circumstances, hard-working mechanics and others, who have embarked on an intellectual pursuit and found something better in life than beer and betting." He has known a brass worker who was a keen astronomer ; a joiner who studied spiders and discovered two new species, and whose knowledge was such that he was consulted by the British Museum experts ; and a cats' meat man who carried about with him " a small microscope and a collection of insects which he was always ready to show to anyone interested."

" A baker's man who used to deliver bread to my house was a numismatist. I had occasion to test his knowledge of coins. I had dug up a small silver piece in my garden at Hampstead. It bore a rose on one side and a thistle on the other. There was no inscription. The British Museum authorities were unable to place it, but this journeyman baker at once informed me that it was a silver penny of the reign of James I. The two devices symbolised the union of Scotland and England, when that King ascended the throne."

These examples of the hobbies and studies of workers call to mind the concluding verses of Browning's *Shop* :—

> " Because a man has shop to mind
>   In time and place, since flesh must live,
> Needs spirit lack all life behind
>   All stray thoughts, fancies fugitive,
>   All loves except what trade can give ?
>
> I want to know a butcher paints,
>   A baker rhymes for his pursuit,
> Candlestick-maker much acquaints
>   His soul with song, or haply mute
>   Blows out his brains upon the flute !
>
> But—shop each day and all day long !
>   Friend, your good angel slept, your star
> Suffered eclipse, fate did you wrong !
>   From where these sorts of treasures are,
>   There should our hearts be—Christ, how far !"

It is often the apparently busiest men and women who find time for hobbies and studies. They always know of something to turn to in spare moments, and are never ' at a loose end.'

Mr. Rogers himself says of his own experience :—

" Such time as I have devoted to my hobbies has been the leisure after business hours. Often I am asked ' How do you find time to do all this work ? ' The answer is that I *make* time. I do not fritter away my leisure in idleness. I have always some work in hand that I can turn to when a wet evening keeps me indoors."

There are, no doubt, and we have already given examples,[1] workers who have no energy to spare after a day's exhausting or irksome labour. But there are many more, and in the future there are likely to be an increasing number, who have a considerable space of leisure with energy to fill it, if they were trained to occupy fruitfully the time that they often find ' hanging on their hands.' That is why so many workers eagerly welcome and make use of the facilities for leisure training that are offered by the Workers Educational Association, the L.C.C. Institutes, the Y.M.C.A., or Y.W.C.A., Women's Institutes, Community Councils and Educational Settlements. Others who cannot attend classes because they are isolated or work on awkward ' shifts ' or are perhaps too timid to join with others, turn to the wireless or to correspondence courses. Among my Correspondence students many have spoken of the value that the method of postal study has meant to them in opening up new interests and a wider horizon.

Many of them find, often by chance in the course of their study and as a result of the practice and training that the regular production of their essays gives to them, that they have abilities in writing—in prose or in verse—which they had never suspected. An Ayrshire girl telegraph clerk who sent me a delicately written lyric said that she would never have dared to tell anyone in her family or

---

[1] *Supra,* chap. XII.

among her fellow-workers that she had written a poem. Others, gaining confidence and courage from their practice in writing, have written plays or short stories, and have been pleasantly surprised when a publisher accepted them. One of my unseen correspondents, Mr. Simon Evans, a rural postman in Shropshire, has published two delightful books describing the sights and sounds, the characters and the happenings, of the Shropshire country-side.[1] Another, Mr. George Thomas, a young fellow hopelessly crippled with progressive muscular atrophy, whose mother, and a brother and sister, are afflicted with the same disease, has set down a year's diary of his life in a slum tenement looking on to Berwick Market.[2] This undiscourageable cripple spends his time in writing and in composing jazz songs and music. " Writing," (he says), " never did more for a human being than it has done, and is still doing, for me."

It is a surprise to many people to find that a miner writes novels or paints pictures, that a tram-conductor or a telegraph girl writes poems, that a postman reads Greek, or a grocer's assistant studies the philosophy of Spinoza.

Yet the examples I have given, and I can vouch for every one of them, can be matched by countless others from the experience of those who are working in the Adult Education Movement. In Residential Colleges and Educational Settlements, in Tutorial Classes and Women's Institutes, in wireless groups and drama groups and study circles, in the Unemployed Men's Clubs that are springing up to-day all over the country, there are men and women with artistic talent and craftsmanship who are finding a new meaning and motive in life. They are acquiring interests and skills that supplement those of their ordinary employment and even help to compensate to some extent for unemployment.

Some years ago I served with others on a Commission

---

[1] See *Round about the Crooked Steeple*, and *At Abdon Burf*.
[2] See *A Tenement in Soho*.

set up by the British Institute of Adult Education to consider the educational possibilities of the Settlement movement, in view of the fact that many of the older Social Settlements were taking on Adult Educational work, and at the same time a number of new Educational Settlements were springing up in various parts of the country.

At one of the meetings of the Commission I outlined my ideal of a Utopian Public House, and it served to suggest to the other members some of the features that an educational club-house should possess. In the Report that was published we proposed that in each town and village there should be an Adult Education Community Centre or ' Guildhouse ' with a resident warden or wardens, where adult students could find all the facilities of an educational club.

" The Guildhouse then should provide comfortable and adequate accommodation for all its activities in a building which is, by preference, simple in its design and decoration. It ought to suggest the University rather than the school, the club and not the committee room. If it is bare and dull it cannot fulfil its own educative function. On the other hand, if it is elaborate it will repel many of those for whose use it is primarily intended. Its purpose is to serve as the common home and hearth of all those in the community who care for books, pictures, and music, for fine handicraft, for group study and informal discussion. In addition to whatever number of small, comfortably furnished class-rooms may be required, a common-room, or lounge, with facilities for obtaining well-served light refreshment, is indispensable. A library (on the open access principle), and a hall for public lectures, concerts and dramatic performances, are in the highest degree desirable. In many communities members of tutorial classes cannot always find at home the quiet needed for reading and essay writing : a library where they can do their work in comfort is a real boon. In cities the value of a garden is considerable for both rest and recreation, and the members will probably take their share in its upkeep. Many members will desire a workshop where they can satisfy their instinct for craftsmanship, without being tied down to strict courses of technical instruction, and their curiosity, by experiments in the making of wireless and other scientific apparatus. Many who take an interest in music will wish for a special music room where all the necessary facilities and opportunities for practising instrumental or vocal music can be obtained without disturbing the activities or comfort of others. In planning a Guildhouse provision for physical education might well be given careful consideration.[1]

Since that Report was issued the number of Educational Settlements has steadily increased, while in addition, first in the distressed areas, and now all over the country, the unemployment crisis has brought into being Unemployed Workers' Clubs and Occupation Centres.[2]

I believe that many of these Clubs and Occupation Centres will find a permanent place and a valuable function when the present crisis is past, as Community Centres in which workers of all kinds can obtain facilities for training in leisure occupations. For all of us alike, employed and unemployed, want a new kind of recreation that shall engage more of the whole man's interest than is liable to be aroused by a game, a show, or what we significantly call a ' pastime.' It is the whole man that must be catered for—his body, by exercises of a kind that do more than keep him ' fit ' for something else : his mind

[1] *The Guildhouse*, p. 6o, published by the British Institute of Adult Education.

[2] See *Unemployment and Opportunity*, published by the National Council of Social Service, and *The Unemployed Service Bulletin*, published by the Central Advisory Council for Unemployed Workers for the British Institute of Adult Education.

by interests that absorb him so fully that he will never be at a loss what to do. This is what Dr. Jacks calls 'the Higher Recreation,' which "includes all the beautiful skills, crafts and hobbies that human beings can practise, on and up to the finest of the fine arts."[1] In many books and articles he has been preaching for some time the gospel of a new kind of recreation and of a new kind of education, on the ground that education should be recreative and recreation educative. Certainly the test of a good education is what it leads people to do with themselves in their leisure time, and the Adult Education movement exists to give to men and women a capacity for filling their lives with happy and fruitful occupations which their earlier education or lack of education has failed to yield.

It might seem at first sight that the organisation of leisure was a contradiction in terms, since leisure is by definition the time that we spend in our own way and on our own initiative. But just as the play of children loses nothing of its freshness and spontaneity when it is guided in organised games by judicious and unobtrusive suggestion and leadership, so the leisure of adults may gain from the guidance and direction of groups who are not only able to provide the best facilities for leisure occupations but also to foster the corporate life and atmosphere which enhance and reinforce individual effort. We must, however, guard against over-organisation. It is possible so to organise people's leisure that they never have any time to themselves to be really leisurely, " to stand and stare." Over-organisation here, as elsewhere, defeats its own end. Many of us are already in danger of losing one of the most valuable features of leisure—the opportunity of mental relaxation, which, as Professor Graham Wallas reminded us in his *Art of Thought*, affords one of the best conditions for the ' incubation ' of new ideas, and the inspiration of creative art. Yet organisa-

---

[1] *Education through Recreation*, p. 102.

tion and some State assistance may be usefully encouraged if confined to the provision of facilities and kept free from undue pressure or unsuitable propaganda. We may well take suggestions from some of the activities of the Italian *Opera Nazionale Dopolavoro* or National Institute for the Use of Leisure, with its travelling cinemas under *L'Unione Cinematografica Educativa* (L.U.C.E.), and perambulating theatres, and its encouragement of the *Balilla* or Youth Movement in cultural and physical education.[1] We shall wish to avoid the party propaganda that turns these activities to Fascist purposes in Italy, or similar activities to Communist ends in Russia. We have in this country no Ministry of Fine Arts, and we shall not perhaps wish to set up a Ministry of Leisure alongside our Ministry of Labour. But none the less there is much that may be done to stimulate the arts and improve the standard of the theatres, the opera, the wireless, and the films. Organisations like the British Drama League and the recently established National Film Institute are helping to this end. In open air pursuits the National Playing Fields Association and the Youth Hostels Association are extending facilities for sports and hiking, while the Society for the Preservation of Rural England stands guard against the Vandal.

In conclusion I would suggest that the arrangement and enjoyment of leisure is an art that needs careful thought and preparation. The art of life indeed consists largely in the capacity to spend wisely and happily the hours in which we are most free—free from the demands and behests of others, free to plan our own activities in and at our own time. To waste those moments is to waste something extraordinarily precious. One of the most horrible and insensate forms of cruelty is killing time.

Let me not be misunderstood. I am not suggesting that rest and relaxation or recreation (bodily or mental) are a waste of time. There are worse abuses of time than

[1] See Cicely Hamilton. *Modern Italy.*

either rest or sport. To name but one, there is idle gossip, which is the very degradation of the art of conversation.

We often speak of the margin of leisure. We may remind ourselves of the wide or narrow margin of a piece of writing or the pages of a book. Sometimes there is little or no margin in which to write one's comments or suggestions. But when the margin is wide what do we do with it ? Sometimes, as in the essays or examination papers that some of us have to read, the margin must be filled with corrections or comments in blue pencil or red ink. So when the daily text of life is poor and mean, the margin of leisure must be used to correct and readjust it.

But the ideal perhaps is to be found in one of those old illuminated manuscripts of the Middle Ages that you may see in the Bodleian Library—and that belong to the days (though I do not say the good old days) before the age of the machine. The big black letters of the small space of text are surrounded by beautiful and delicate pictures and decorations—brightly coloured scrolls and leaves or flowers, or landscapes and portraits that illustrate and illuminate the text. And in Utopia the margin of leisure will be wide and full of beauty, if indeed the text and the margin are distinguishable, and a man's leisure will illuminate and illustrate his work. For work and play, industry and art will have come together, craftsmanship will complete the work of the machine, and the machine the work of craftsmanship, leisure will complete the life of work, and work complete the life of leisure.

"In my heaven," says Father Keegan in *John Bull's Other Island*, " all work is play, and all play is life, three in one and one in three."

Till then, we must prize what margin of leisure is vouchsafed to us, and fill it with what fancies most delight us and are most likely in their turn to delight our fellow men.

CHAPTER XV

WRITERS like Oswald Spengler and Signora Ferrero (Gina Lombroso) have prophesied the decline of Western civilisation as a result of man's worship of mechanism.[1] It is clear that there is no possibility of going back to pre-machine conditions, even if we wish to do so, and that we must admit with Samuel Butler that the mischief, if it be a mischief, " is already done."[2] Spengler believes that we are approaching an ultimate catastrophe, and calls on us to prepare to meet our doom with dignity. Signora Ferrero thinks there is still time to call a halt, and to restore something of the older values by the building up of small groups of co-operative producers in agriculture and the crafts who will learn to distinguish the use of the machine from the abuse of ' machinism.' There are many who would like to escape from the prison-like organisation of the ' great industry ' as René Clair's hero escapes from the mass-production gramophone factory which he directs, in *A Nous La Liberté*. With his prison comrade he takes singing to the open road. But this is parable and satire, and not practical advice. Others point to more hopeful possibilities to be won, not by turning back, but by going forward, with a new purpose and constructive plans.

" We are, if we could but grapple with our fate, the most fortunate of the generations of men. In a single lifetime Science has given us more power over Nature, and extended further the range of vision of the exploring mind, than in all recorded history. Now, and now only,

---

[1] See Spengler's *Decline of the West*, and *Man and Technics ;* and Gina Lombroso's *Tragedia del Progresso* (French translation : *La Rançon du Machinisme*).

[2] cf. *supra*, p. 10.

our material resources, technical knowledge and industrial skill, are enough to afford to every man of the world's teeming population physical comfort, adequate leisure, and access to everything in our rich heritage of civilisation that he has the personal quality to enjoy. We need but the regulative wisdom to control our specialised activities and the thrusting energy of our sectional and selfish interests."[1]

" If we could but grapple with our fate "—-Have we the wisdom and the will to do it ? Sir Alfred Ewing, a veteran of engineering science, in his Presidential Address to the British Association in 1932, expressed his profound misgivings.

" An old exponent of applied mechanics may be forgiven if he expresses something of the disillusion with which, now standing aside, he watches the sweeping pageant of discovery and invention in which he used to take unbounded delight. It is impossible not to ask, whither does this tremendous procession tend ? What, after all, is its goal ? What its probable influence upon the future of the human race ? We are acutely aware that the engineer's gifts have been and may be grievously abused. In some there is potential tragedy as well as present burden. Man is ethically unprepared for so great a bounty. In the slow evolution of morals he is still unfit for the tremendous responsibility it entails. The command of Nature has been put into his hands before he knows how to command himself."[2]

It is this ethical preparation of insight and control of which we stand in need if we are to turn to good account the powers of which we have come into possession.

" Man has been more successful in learning to control his environment than in learning to control his social relationships ; in learning to co-operate with wind and

[1] Epilogue to Salter's *Recovery*, p. 302.
[2] *The Times*, Sept. 1st, 1932.

water than in learning to co-operate with his fellow-men."[1]

It is not the machine that is responsible for our misfortunes and misdeeds. The fault is not in the machine, but " in ourselves, that we are underlings." The machine has neither power nor will of its own to help or hinder. It stands ready to serve the ends that we choose to pursue. But we use or misuse it at our peril. If we turn it on ourselves in the internecine conflict of mechanised warfare, we misuse it for our destruction instead of using it for our welfare. If we squander on it with prodigious wastefulness our natural resources—of coal and oil, of copper and iron and timber[2]—we are preparing once again our own destruction. If we lay waste the countryside and despoil its beauty and disturb its quiet, it is we who are the Vandals. Finally, if we seek personal power and profit by the exploitation of others—our fellow countrymen or far-off native races—it is on us and not on the machine that the curse of Midas will descend.

But the very fact that we are troubled in our minds and visited with these misgivings is itself our hope. The world depression has shocked us all into asking ourselves the obvious but ultimate questions which are too seldom asked because they are so obvious. We invent more and more wonderful machines : What for ? We move about more and more rapidly : What for ? We organise more and more elaborately : What for ? We produce more and more goods : What for ? What, after all, is industry for ? Was industry made for man, or man for industry ? If industry was made for man, it must be adapted to his needs as worker and consumer. If the machine was made for man, it must be made the servant and not the master of his life. The spirit is more powerful than the machine, and must control and direct its energies.

---

[1] Hammond. *The Skilled Labourer*, p. 381.
[2] See Chase. *Men and Machines*, ch. xvi ; Lombroso : *La Rançon du Machinisme*, p. 223.

O*

We need to look at the whole world of industry with
fresh eyes, to ask ourselves again what we want to produce,
and how we can best employ our powers in producing it,
to the end that the work and its results may alike satisfy
human capacities and human·needs. In the foregoing
chapters we have considered some of the steps that may be
taken to see that the conditions of labour are designed to
promote the interest and welfare of the worker ; and
also some of the measures that are required to secure that
the wealth which machinery places at our disposal may
be distributed for the benefit of all. We have also
envisaged the possibilities of fuller leisure and the preparation that is needed to equip men for its enjoyment.
But the greatest need of all is a preparation of the mind and
spirit that shall refine our standards of judgment and of
taste, revise our false values, and purify and simplify our
desires. For it is we, the consumers, who make the final
and determining demands that set the wheels of the
machine in motion.

END